Edward Balfour

The Agricultural Pests of India, and of Eastern and Southern Asia

Edward Balfour

The Agricultural Pests of India, and of Eastern and Southern Asia

ISBN/EAN: 9783743393288

Manufactured in Europe, USA, Canada, Australia, Japa

Cover: Foto ©Suzi / pixelio.de

Manufactured and distributed by brebook publishing software
(www.brebook.com)

Edward Balfour

The Agricultural Pests of India, and of Eastern and Southern Asia

THE

AGRICULTURAL PESTS OF INDIA,

AND OF

EASTERN AND SOUTHERN ASIA,

VEGETABLE AND ANIMAL,

INJURIOUS TO MAN AND HIS PRODUCTS.

BY

SURGEON GENERAL EDWARD BALFOUR,

CORRESPONDING MEMBER OF THE IMPERIAL-ROYAL GEOLOGICAL INSTITUTE, VIENNA;
FELLOW OF THE MADRAS UNIVERSITY;

AUTHOR OF

'THE CYCLOPÆDIA OF INDIA AND OF EASTERN AND SOUTHERN ASIA,'
'THE TIMBER TREES OF INDIA AND OF EASTERN AND SOUTHERN ASIA,' ETC.;

FOUNDER OF THE GOVERNMENT CENTRAL MUSEUM, MADRAS;
OF THE MYSORE MUSEUM, BANGALORE; ETC.

LONDON:
BERNARD QUARITCH, 15 PICCADILLY.
1887.

PREFATORY REMARKS.

THE blights and murrains of India have hitherto had their only record in the pages of journals and newspapers, or occasionally in official reports; but, as the correspondence below will show, effect has now been given to my recommendation to have periodical reports on occurring pests, reports are coming to hand, and the need for a more accessible registry has suggested this book.

The expediency of having the text illustrated by plates and wood engravings is under consideration.

EDWARD BALFOUR.

31*st March* 1887.

From Surgeon General Edward Balfour to the Under Secretary of State for India.

2 OXFORD SQUARE, HYDE PARK, LONDON,
8*th August* 1885.

SIR,—The article ' Insects ' in the 3rd edition of the *Cyclopædia of India and of Eastern and Southern Asia,* is, I think, the first attempt to give a general view of the entomology of that wide region. This is, in many ways, a very difficult branch of natural history; but this article was prepared and printed by me under the care of two scientific men, one of them ranking among the most learned of living entomologists, and I was favoured also with counsel from Miss Ormerod, who, in this country, annually reports on the insects injurious to food crops, forest trees, and fruits, and the prevention of insect ravages.

The like of Miss Ormerod's form of reporting has never been done for India, although every year to some extent, and from time to time largely, losses occur there from the pests which attack agricultural produce. India has hitherto been remiss in this matter, contenting itself with references as to individual insects or blights to such persons as were thought likely to be able to give information. But the subject is of far too great importance to agricultural India to be left to be treated in so casual a manner, and the special knowledge now available might be utilized to describe the insects which injure the agricultural, horticultural, and forest produce of India, suggesting means of preventing, and remedies for same.

The reports should be restricted rigidly to the injurious insects, and should be half-yearly, to fit in with the two great agricultural seasons.—I have, etc.,

EDWARD BALFOUR, *Surgeon General.*

To Surgeon General Edward Balfour, 2 Oxford Square, Hyde Park, W.

INDIA OFFICE,
24th September 1885.

SIR,—I am directed by the Secretary of State for India in Council to acknowledge with thanks your letter of the 8th ultimo, with reference to the preparation of official annual reports on the insects destructive to crops and forests in India; and to inform you in reply that a copy of it has been forwarded to the Government of India.—I am, etc.,   HORACE WALPOLE.

To *Horace Walpole, Esq., C.B.*

2 OXFORD SQUARE, HYDE PARK, W.,
28th September 1885.

DEAR SIR,—I sent to Miss Ormerod copy of my letter of the 8th August, and copy of the Secretary of State's letter of 24th instant in reply.

I enclose now copy of the acknowledgment of these which Miss Ormerod has written to me.

I beg the favour of your submitting to Her Majesty's Secretary of State that if this correspondence could be printed and circulated from here, all the entomologists and their entomological societies in all Europe could aid in this very important investigation. There are only a very few in India. I have no doubt but that I could distribute usefully 200 copies.—I am, etc.,

EDWARD BALFOUR.

To *Surgeon General Edward Balfour*, 2 *Oxford Square, W.*

DUNSTER LODGE, SPRING GROVE, ISLEWORTH,
25th September 1885.

DEAR MR. BALFOUR,—I am very much obliged to you for favouring me with a copy of your letter to the Under Secretary of State for India relative to the importance of acquiring serviceable information regarding the injurious crop insects of India, and also kindly giving me a copy of the official reply.

I do not see that you could do better, as a commencement, than thus bring the subject shortly and clearly forward ; and, as far as I can form an opinion, I think that the course you suggest would be the constant means of saving thousands of pounds yearly—occasionally (perhaps more than occasionally) of saving millions. I found this opinion, of course, on consideration of the unremunerative outlay so often occurring on some of the great crops, notably (as coming specially under my notice) the loss by ravage of coffee-plant grubs.

The information that is needed could be given by plain and simple jotting down by various persons of what they themselves have observed.

One man notices, perhaps, how deep the grubs go ; another, how long they live ; and so, by collating the points, we get to know the whole history of habits, which is what is needed to work on. It may take a few years to get the whole life history of the insects, but we soon get in the way mentioned above (on which plan my own reports are formed) to learn the main points, and then all observers are requested to find the missing part of the history.

If reports were formed in this way, there would very shortly be a great increase of useful knowledge throughout the Indian empire.

I present my reports yearly to the contributors, thus they take a personal interest in the work, and, what is immensely important in things of this kind, the book comes to them on publication ; they have not the trouble of ordering it. The expense would be a mere nothing to Government, seeing that I, a private individual, have now for eight years, without the slightest assistance, carried on the work in England.

The great mistake is in waiting until attack is unusually destructive, and then consulting those who, though eminently skilled in classification of insects, have no idea or well - founded knowledge of the points of agricultural treatment or forestry which must be brought to bear on the insects in some special stage of their life. Likewise (as occurred not long ago) to advise reliance on the insectivorous animals of England for help in India or Ceylon is a decided mistake.

If, from the long experience which I have now had of gaining information on insect attacks and forming it into readable shape, you think any suggestions on my part would be of service, I should be most happy to give any attention in my power to the subject. But, meanwhile, I may most truly say that if the crop, or timber, or fruit growers of India were furnished with plain and comprehensive accounts of the history and habits of the common insect pests, accompanied by woodcut figures, so as to convey the appearance of the pests without wearisome description of details, that all this would be a national benefit, soon paying the outlay hundreds of times over. — With renewed thanks, I am, dear Mr. Balfour, yours very truly,

ELEANOR A. ORMEROD.

P.S.—Pray make any use you may think fit of this ; it will give me pleasure for it to be of any service.

E. A. O.

To Surgeon General E. Balfour, 2 Oxford Square,
Hyde Park, W.

INDIA OFFICE,
4th November 1885.

SIR,—I am directed by the Secretary of State for India in Council to acknowledge with thanks the receipt of your letter of 28th September last, enclosing an interesting communication from Miss Ormerod on the subject of the insect pests of Indian crops and forests. In reply, I am to inform you that a copy of this correspondence has been forwarded to the Government of India ; and that another copy of it, and of your previous letter of the 8th August last, has been sent to the Society of Arts, for publication in their widely circulated *Journal.*—I am, Sir, your obedient servant,

J. A. GODLEY.

THE AGRICULTURAL PESTS OF INDIA.

AGRICULTURAL PESTS are the foes of man. The injuries which they inflict on man, on the products he has reared, and on the animals he has domesticated, are observable in every - day life, in the field, the garden, the poultry yard, the horse and cattle sheds, the sheep pens, and elephant and camel karkhānas. No country is free from them, but in British India there are conditions peculiarly favouring their presence.

The census of 1881 showed its population to be 198,790,853 souls, of whom 69,952,747 were agriculturists, 220,803 horticulturists, 35,076 arboriculturists, and 990,342 were tending animals.

In 1884 − 85 the revenue of British India was Rs. 70,69,06,810, of which the land - tax yielded Rs. 21,83,22,110 ; Rs. 8,81,64,690 were derived from opium, and Rs. 98,69,840 from forest. In that year 22,425 human beings were killed by elephants, tigers, leopards, wolves, bears, hyænas, and venomous snakes ; and of cattle killed the number was 49,987. The numbers engaged in agriculture, the great revenue obtained from the lands, and the losses the people are exposed to from wild beasts, all indicate the need for protective measures ; and there has been a beginning made :—

In Ceylon, Travancore, Bengal, Burmah, and Siam, arrangements have been made by the respective Governments for snaring elephants ; also in India rewards of a hundred rupees and upwards are given for killing tigers and man-eating leopards, with smaller sums for killing snakes; also, as anthrax, epizootic aphtha, dysentery, and rinderpest carry off the cattle of the cultivators in great numbers, how to ward off these murrains has been a subject of serious thought. In the early part of this century, the pioneer on this line of economic research, Dr. Gilchrist, of the Madras Medical Service, wrote *A Practical Treatise on the Treatment of the Diseases of the Elephant, Camel, and Horned Cattle, with Instructions for Preserving their Efficiency*, and ever since then the diseases of these animals have been receiving the attention of the Commissariat and Veterinary Depart-ments. The Madras Government has recently appointed an inspector, deputy-inspector, and local inspectors of cattle diseases. This is a useful step, because these domestic animals are the Indian husbandman's sole wealth. But the pecuniary losses from the ravages of animal and vegetable pests on the cultivated products of the country have never yet been made the subject of general inquiry, although seemingly their extent, even in comparatively favourable years, may be estimated at a large share of the gross revenue of the country. A subject of such moment might well have received early attention. Hitherto, however, India has been contenting itself with making references as to individual insects or blights to such persons as may have been deemed likely to furnish information regarding them. But the subject is of far too great importance to be treated in so casual a manner; and in 1885 I suggested that the special knowledge now available might be utilized to describe the insects which injure the agricultural, horticultural, and forest produce of India. Her Majesty's Secretary of

State forwarded on that letter to the Government of India, and sent a copy of it to the *Journal of the Society of Arts*, in which it appeared on the 13th of November 1885, with an accompanying letter from Miss Ormerod supporting my views. The extent to which agricultural produce is destroyed by animal and vegetable pests may receive a few illustrations. The annual crop of cotton of British India may be estimated at 6,419,718 cwt., valued at seven crores of rupees. I have seen, I think in the *Zoologist*, a statement by the United States Agricultural Commissioner, to the effect that in parts of India one-fourth of the cotton crop is sometimes lost from the ravages of the larvæ of one insect, the Depressaria gossipiella. In Ceylon the loss to the coffee planters from several tiny vegetable and animal pests was great ; but that industry was finally ruined by a fungus, the Hemileia vastatrix, which spread through the island and the plantations in the Peninsula. Mr. Thiselton Dyer, in a letter dated Kew, 12th January 1881, addressed to the Colonial Office, mentions as an estimate by the Rev. R. Abbay for the five years up to 1871, that the average yield of coffee in Ceylon had been 4·5 cwt. per acre, whilst for the five succeeding years the average had been only 2·2 cwt. Also, that for the ten years 1869 to 1878, Mr. Abbay had estimated the total loss due to the leaf disease at from £12,000,000 to £15,000,000. The 'Acreage under Coffee' after 1870* had decreased

					Acreage under Coffee.
* 1870,	.	.	.	.	203,909
1871,	.	.	.	.	196,881½
1872,	.	.	.	.	182,342
1873,	.	.	.	.	177,980
1884,	.	.	.	.	231,976
1885,	.	.	.	.	192,434

somewhat, but nothing to account for the crop falling off to half the previous yield.

India and Ceylon agriculturists are not solitary sufferers. In England the annual yield of the hop plantations, as the *Edinburgh Review* tells us, is about 7 cwt. per acre. But a serious blight occurred in 1882, and it was estimated that the whole produce of the hop land in England (65,619 acres) did not exceed 114,839 cwt., or an average yield of $1\frac{3}{4}$ cwt. per acre. The injury inflicted on the hop growers in that year by the hop aphis (Aphis humuli), one of the ten different genera of insects that attack the hops, amounted to the value of £2,700,000.

Russia has not escaped. The yield of its corn crops sunk from the rate of 8·3 bushels per acre in 1875 to that of 5·1 bushels per acre in 1883, from the ravages of insect swarms.

In France the phylloxera, which has infested the vineyard in 53 departments, made its first appearance in 1865, and was reported on in 1884. The vineyard surface existing before the malady was 2,485,829 hectares, but at the time of the 1884 report it was reduced to 2,056,713 hectares. Measured by the production of wine, the yield of 1874 was 63,000,000 hectolitres. In 1879 it sank to less than 26,000,000, but in 1884 it recovered to 35,000,000.

The Commissioner of Agriculture for the United States has mentioned in his report of 1874 (page 164) that their annual losses of cotton from ravages of cotton insects amount possibly to half a million bales in years of insect prevalence. One-fourth of a million bales, he says, would be deemed a light infliction, and yet, at $100 per bale, such a loss would be equivalent to $25,000,000. Again,

we are told of the Diplosis tritici, the wheat midge of
North America, that in 1854, in New York alone, it
destroyed the wheat crop to the value of £3,000,000.
In Ohio, in the same year, it was still more hurtful; and
in Canada it destroyed 8,000,000 bushels of wheat.
Later on, in 1864, the cash value of the wheat and corn
destroyed in the State of Illinois by the chinch bug was
estimated at $73,000,000. Still more recently, in 1882,
when the total public revenue of the United States was
$524,000,000, the annual value of the agricultural
produce consumed by insects has been estimated, at the
lowest, at $200,000,000, and by Mr. R. D. Walsh at
$300,000,000.

For some years past the Governments of India have
been recommending to the people improved implements
of husbandry, but the above details will have shown
that protection against animal and vegetable raiders is a
great, it may be even a greater, want. To make these
enemies known, and to indicate measures likely to check
their ravages, are the objects in view in publishing this
volume. The larger quadrupeds are becoming fewer
under the hand of man, but there are other foes preying
on the produce of the fields, and husbandmen may
legitimately look to their rulers for counsel how to defeat
these enemies, and secure for the increasing population
a larger share of the crops. In so praiseworthy a pursuit
agricultural India might reasonably hope for help from
some of its own people, and they may certainly trust to
the learned men of Europe and America for all the aid
that science can afford. I have already to acknowledge
valued assistance from the library, the entomological, and
the botanical departments of the British Museum of
Natural History, and the library of the Colonial Office as

to Ceylon. Professor Westwood, of the Oxford University Museum, in January 1885, revised what I had then written as to destructive insects; and Mr. Waterhouse, of the British Museum, revised nearly the whole in manuscript and the proofs as they passed through the press. The article ' Coleoptera ' is from his pen, and that on ' Fishes ' is chiefly by Dr. Francis Day, C.I.E.

The alphabetical arrangement has been adopted for the contents, that being deemed the most suitable form in the present state of our knowledge.

The people of India are skilled in the use of all the implements of husbandry, and in applying manures economically, although in the latter they are far excelled by the Chinese. But in protecting their crops and in cleanly cultivation, India is greatly behind.

One of the protective measures against insect ravages, which is strongly urged on cultivators in all countries, is to change the crops in successive years. Each insect species has its own particular plants on which alone it lives, and when deprived of food by a change in cultivation, they die. The cucumbers, the rice and cotton plants, the tea and coffee shrubs, the bamboo, the sāl, pine, and fir trees, have each their own enemies; and on land where a rotation of crops is followed, the parasites have to seek fresh marauding ground once a twelve-month or oftener, and are frequently kept away entirely or for a considerable period by an absence of their special food. Mr. Scott says that a steady system of rotation of cereals generally with the pulses, would to a certainty impair the fecundity of the chief ravagers of the food crops,—the grub, maggot, and caterpillar forms,—as few of the insects with which the cultivated crops have to contend find a common food-stuff on the cereals and pulses. A large percentage of them would thus be destroyed from season to season, before they reached their particular food-stuff.

Man may enlist the aid of the natural enemies of these marauders. All insectivorous creatures should be encouraged and protected. Of birds may be named crows, shrikes, woodpeckers, titmice, jays, starlings, lapwings, plovers, domestic fowls, and guinea-fowls. Insects are kept under by all the woodpeckers, conspicuously the Chrysocolaptes sultaneus, Chrysonotus Shorei, and Brachypternus aurantius. The eggs and larvæ of insects are the natural food of the Sittinæ or nut-hatches, the Certhias or true creepers, and the Parrinæ or titmice. The hardbodied beetles and other Coleoptera are, in their perfect or imago state, eagerly seized while on the wing by shrikes, drongos, crows, rollers, bee-eaters, thrushes, etc. The crow and the myna are the incessant foes of the cricket and grasshopper family. The Cheiroptera, bats, the Insectivora carnaria, and the Viverra, civets, are all insect feeders, and render valuable service to man.

The Acari and Ichneumonidæ are destructive to caterpillars and grubs; the ichneumons destroy the larvæ of many species of gall-flies. The lady-bird beetles, species of Coccinella, are natural enemies of the aphides. The families Chalcididæ, Crabronidæ, and Proctotrupidæ are parasites. Aphides or plant-lice can be kept under by squirting a solution of soft soap mixed with a decoction of quassia. Traps may be used for caterpillars, baited with their favourite food; fires may be lighted to stifle insects with the smoke; the cockchafer (Melolontha vulgaris) may be attracted by a lantern and intercepted with a small mesh net. The adjutant birds, Leptoptilos argala and L. Javanica, and the mongoos, Herpestes griseus, are the foes of snakes, and are protected in India ; and India has now a close season for some birds and mammals.

Some plants are known to have protecting qualities. Linnæus, writing of the primrose, says, ' Sheep and goats eat it, cows are not fond of it, horses and swine refuse it.' Mr. Scott tells us that while other crops suffered, various umbellifers, which are cultivated in India for their aromatic properties, as the Anethum sowa, Coriandrum sativum, Fœniculum panmori, F. vulgaris, Petroselinum sativum, and Ptychotis ajowan, had a complete exemption from insects of all kinds. A crop of white mustard kills or. scares the wire-worm. Dill grown in cabbage beds protects the cabbages from caterpillars. The Sesamum indicum is afforded protection from insect attacks by the presence of glands, which, as yielding a sweet secretion, are sedulously haunted by a common ant. W. Bancroft, writing in 1878, mentioned that he had with advantage sown the Dolichos lablab and Cajanus Indicus pulse among the sugar-cane fields, for the purpose of attracting the ichneumon flies which destroy the cane louse. Frogs avoid localities where valerian is grown, and the hellebore is said to have protective virtues. The Dekhan ryots protect their crops from deer by sowing safflower as an edging of their fields. As to crickets, free irrigation brings them to the surface of the soil and makes the grasshoppers skip out from their leafy harbourings. Thinning, weeding, watering, hand-picking, and dusting with quicklime and wood-ashes or soot, are useful means of keeping them under. Pyrethrum carneum, *Biebers ;* P. roseum, *Biebers ;* and P. Willemoti, *Duchartre,* plants of the Caucasus, merit cultivation in India. The United States Patent Office Report for 1862 declared the powdered leaves to be superior to camphor, pepper, or other insect destroyer. The powder is used pure, or mixed with ten to twenty times its bulk of wood-ashes or flour. It is useful against insects injurious to agriculture, horticulture, and domestic economy; useful to protect wool, furs, and feathers, collections of natural history, as mammals, birds, fishes, reptiles, and chiefly against weevils, beetles, crickets, roaches, moths, wheat-flies, fleas, maggots, midges, plant-lice, earwigs, spiders, ants, etc., alike in their larva form and as perfect insects. It is recommended to be blown on plants in the field, hot-house, and conservatory, by means of bellows; to be dusted and blown into walls and furniture, and sprinkled upon feathers, furs, and woollens. In Southern Dalmatia, the powder of the straight-leaved pepper-wort, Lepidium ruderale, *Linn.*, is used against fleas. In Southern Russia, Aristolochia clematitis, *Linn.*, is used against bugs. In the United States, the powder of the wood of Cedrela odorata is used against all noxious insects.

Cleanly farming is an indispensable duty in all efforts that may be made to keep away insects. Granaries and store-rooms, walls and floors and rafters, should be carefully brushed and washed with hot water, and all the sweepings and dust burnt.

Many weevils are impatient of light, and are destroyed in stored grain by frequently turning it over, and occasionally running it through a winnowing machine. Sprinkling powdered camphor in the store also kills or disperses them. Cultivators should remove all dead wood, all withered branches and shoots, and all the bark from stakes, posts, and palings; burning all unrequired chaff, all infected branches, all stubble, rubbish, and all field and barn refuse. Dead leaves and other vegetable substances, not thoroughly and completely decayed, are almost sure to introduce destructive fungi. Manure heaps should be kept aloof from the neighbourhood of infected places, and suspected manure turned and treated with lime. Beat all hedges and keep all ditches clean. Keep land free from weeds, remove grass all round fruit trees, and all of it from orchards. Kerosene, paraffine, and petroleum have all been found of use. They can be mixed with earth, ashes, or sawdust, and sprinkled on infected beds of vegetables, or a kerosene solution may be thrown on plants with a syringe. For the latter mode of applying it, it is made into an emulsion, diluted with water, and used at once; for if allowed to stand the component parts separate. Kerosene, one quart; milk, twelve ounces; emulsify by active churning. For use, dilute with twelve to twenty times of water. Or, take soft soap, one quart; water, one gallon; bring to a boil. Add one gallon kerosene to twelve gallons soap solution. Many other substances have been recommended to be used to check mischievous insects,—the other hydro-carbons, paraffine, and petroleum, also tar, gas-water, ashes, soot, quicklime, lime, and camphor. The stems of plants and bushes near the ground are advised to be painted with limewash; sulphates of iron and copper and nitrate of soda are also used.

A

Acarina. An order of insects of the class Arachnoidea. Their species are the mites. The families are arranged by naturalists as follows :—

Tetranychidæ, spinning mites.

Trombidiidæ, harvest mites.

B'dellidæ, snouted harvest mites.

Hydrachnidæ, water mites.

Gamasidæ, insect mite parasites.

Ixodidæ, ticks.

Halacaridæ, marine mites.

Oribatidæ, beetle mites.

Acaridæ, true mites, viz. :

1st section, Hypoderidæ, subcutaneous mites.

2nd   „   Hypopodæ, ichneumon mites.

3rd   „   Tyroglyphidæ, cheese mites.

4th   „   Sarcoptidæ, itch and louse mites.

5th   „   Phytoptidæ, gall mites.

Many of this order of insects, the mites, the ticks, the itch and louse, cause much annoyance and discomfort, alike to man and to domesticated and wild animals. Dr. Pereira found the addition of a few drops of acetic acid an effectual remedy against the attacks of the Acarus domesticus mites. Cheese mites are harmless when eaten.

Achæa melicerte, *Hubner,* a moth of the family Dysgoniidæ, occurs in Ceylon, and at Bellary in the Ceded Districts, and was named by Drury Phalæna noctua melicerte. Its larva is called Thondala hoola in Canarese.

They feed on the castor-oil plants, the leaves and flowers
of which they eat; on two or three acres of land, in one
night, they will leave nothing but bare branches. The
plants seldom survive their attack, and at best yield only
one-fourth of the produce. The cultivators drive them
from the plants by smoking; but this is impossible of
application when seeds are sown on an extensive area, in
which case the husbandmen give up all hopes of the
crop. The adult larva has sixteen legs, the first pair of
middle legs aborted; two dorsal red tubercles on twelfth
segment; colour bluish-grey, numerously speckled with
bluish-black; a lateral and sub-lateral yellowish band,
with an intervening bluish-grey line; spiracles and fore-
legs red; a dorsal black stripe, bordered by reddish-white
spots, between fifth and sixth segments; head black
striped. Pupa formed within a leaf.— *W.-M.*

Acheta. A large species of Acheta attacks the casuarina trees. It lodges at the foot of the tree, and at
nightfall ascends the tree and cuts off the young top
shoots.—See Gryllidæ.

Actiniæ and **Medusæ** have more or less urticating
properties. The latter are of the class radiata, and
are commonly known by the name of sea-nettle and
jelly-fish. The Actiniæ are polyps. A cyanea of
Pondicherry secretes an extremely acrid and irritating
fluid. The Physalia, or Portuguese man-of-war, also
causes a considerable amount of irritation, the stinging
sensation continuing for hours. Physalia is a colony, the
individuals of which are called zooids. Some are for
locomotion, others are feeders, and have other purposes,
but they all look alike, the appearance presented being a
blue, entangled, jelly-like mass of threads, coiling, con-
tracting, extending, floated and suspended from a rich

balloon-like bubble. The tentacles are covered with delicate cells, each of which contains a minute coiled dart or lasso, and if a foreign substance come in contact with the tentacles, millions of these weapons are hurled into it, producing a peculiar paralyzing effect.

Agrotis segetum, *Steph., Schiff.* Noctua segetum of India and High Asia. The larva of this moth is the very destructive 'black grub' of the Ceylon coffee planter. This pest is about an inch long, and is most abundant from August to October. The caterpillar lives in the ground, but comes out at night to feed, and is very common and injurious. They attack not only coffee trees, but all sorts of vegetables and flowers, and are very destructive to gardens and in the field, as they eat everything that is artificially raised, despising grass and weeds. They generally appear only on certain fields, and will not go over an estate. The insect is not confined to Ceylon; its ravages are well known in India, at the Cape of Good Hope, and Europe, where it injures the grain and beet-root crops. In Ceylon it only attacks young coffee trees, gnawing off the bark round the stem just above the ground. Where the trees are very small, they are bitten right off, and the tops sometimes partially dragged under the ground, where the grubs may easily be discovered and dislodged. The damage which they inflict on plantations may be estimated when it is mentioned that Mr. Nietner lost through them in one season, in certain fields, as many as 25 per cent. of the young trees he had put down. A. aquilina is a species of High Asia.—*N.*

Alope ocellifera, *Walker* (A. ricini, *Fabr.*), one of the Lepidoptera, is a species of moth belonging to the family Arctiidæ. It occurs in Ceylon, in the Northern Circars and Bengal, and has been described in Mr. Moore's

Lepidoptera of Ceylon, vol. ii. pp. 70–106. In Calcutta, the caterpillar feeds on the castor-oil plant, to which it is said often to do great damage. In the half-year ending 30th June 1886, the caterpillars in three taluqs of the Vizagapatam district caused considerable damage to the crops of Sesamum orientale, Eleusine coracana, Penicillaria spicata, and cotton. In the Vizianagram taluq the value of the Sesamum crop destroyed was estimated at Rs. 20,000; and in parts of the Gajapati-nagram taluq this plant was so badly destroyed that it had to be ploughed up and other crops raised in its stead. Rain fell in June, and the insects appeared soon after. Being innumerable, the endeavours of the people to collect and destroy them proved futile, though the only remedial measures that Mr. Wood-Mason can suggest are for the ryots to destroy as many eggs, caterpillars, cocoons, and moths as possible, and that the castor-oil plant, the natural food, be grown in all waste places. The caterpillars are known to the people as the 'Cumbly poochie,' two Tamil words meaning 'blanket insect,' and the ryots allege that their crops suffer almost every year. The moth measures from $1\frac{1}{2}$ to 2 inches across the extended wings, and from $1\frac{1}{4}$ to $1\frac{1}{2}$ inches from the forehead to the end of the closed wings, the female being the larger. The front wings are greyish-brown, with six cross bands composed of irregular-shaped dark-brown spots edged with pale yellow; the hind wings are red, with some dark-brown spots usually more or less joined together so as to form three cross bands in the female. The head, the thorax, and the legs are greyish-brown; the abdomen is red, with brown spots along the middle of the back and along the sides. The caterpillar is dark brown, with thick bundles of brindled hairs springing from twelve longitudinal rows of warts. The pupa or chrysalis is also dark brown, and it is enclosed in an oval cocoon, strengthened and protected by the probably poisonous hairs of the caterpillar interwoven with the silk.—*W.-M.*

Amœba. Sheep in certain country districts of New South Wales are liable to a disease somewhat resembling epithelial cancer. It is produced by an amœba, which affects the hoofs, lips, and nostrils of sheep and lambs. The epithelium grows with great rapidity, the wool drops off in the parts attacked, and a festering sore is established. In studying the surroundings of the flocks so affected, and by a process of artificial breeding in an aquarium, Dr. Lendenfeld found that the disease is due to an amœba (A. parasitica) which enters into wounds made by the spines of the variegated thistle. This plant grows in profusion about the feeding grounds. The amœba, having gained an entrance through a wound, multiplies very rapidly between the epithelial and horny layers of the hoof. This disease appears very closely to resemble the fungus-foot disease among the natives of the Madura district of India. The amœba reproduces itself by simple division.—*Dr. Lendenfeld in Pro. Linn. Soc., New South Wales.*

Amphistoma conicum, 'cone - shaped fluke.' Very common in the ox, sheep, musk ox, elk, fallow and red deer, goat, etc. Moisture being essential to the development of the fluke-larvæ, sheep cannot be infested so long as they remain on high and dry grounds.

Amphistoma hominis is a parasite afflicting the natives of Assam. It belongs to the trematode or fluke order of helminths.—See Distoma.

Ancylonycha is a genus of the Orthoptera; some species attack the coffee plants of Ceylon.—See Lachnosterna.

Anobium. One species of this genus of beetles is known

as the death-watch, from its making a tapping noise like the ticking of a watch. They feed on old dry wood, etc.— See Book-worm.

Anthrenus.—See Coleoptera; Dermestidæ.

Ants are great destroyers of seeds, fruits, and sugars. Formica saccharivora, the sugar ant, is supposed to get at the saccharine juices of the sugar-cane. The red ant, a species of Myrmica, bites severely. They avoid turmeric powder. They can be attracted into a cocoa-nut shell with the kernel in it, and destroyed. Formica gigas, an ant of the East Indies, has a female an inch long. The Dimya, or great red ant of Ceylon, bites with intense ferocity, and the bite of the Kaddiya, another species, is much dreaded.

Aphidæ or plant-lice are to be seen on almost every plant in the field and garden, and from their numbers cause great injury to cultivated plants. One British species is the hop-fly, Aphis humuli; another of Europe is the destructive vine blight, Phylloxera vastatrix. They live on the leaves and tender shoots of trees, shrubs, and herbaceous plants, which they pierce in order to suck out the juices. Some of the aphides which reside in cases are small Hemiptera, belonging to the subdivision Homoptera, and to the family of the Hymenelytra.

The aphides multiply enormously. Reaumur calculated that five generations proceeding from a single mother, if no obstacle intervened, might give rise to the astounding number of 5,904,900,000 individuals, and some of them cause great loss to growing crops. One of the most curious of their cases is that which is known as the Chinese gall, from Aphis Chinensis, *Bell.* This case grows on the leaves of Distylium racemosum, *Zucc.*, a large tree of Japan, belonging to the family Hamamelida (Decaisne). According to M. Guibourt, it is also developed on the buds of the tree which is commonly called in Japan, Ou-pey-tse, Ou-pei-tse, Woo-pei-tse. Some galls are useful. False galls are found on the Pistacia vera, P. terebintha, and the P. lentiscus. The insect which produces them is the Aphis pistaciæ, *Linn.*, a small black insect, with a roughened thorax, very long legs, and white wings. A species of aphis attacks the cotton plant in India. Aphides are readily destroyed by water charged with metallic iron. The food of the Coccinellæ, lady-birds, consists almost exclusively of aphides. Other aphidivorous insects are numerous minute Hymenoptera, species of the families Cynipidæ, Ichneumonidæ, and Chalcididæ; and among the Neuroptera, species of Chrysopa or golden eyes. On the mango, peach, and other trees of the Calcutta gardens, there is to be seen the sweetish substance known as honey-dew, supposed to be an excrementitious deposit from aphides. To remove it, syringing with water, or soft soap and water, is recommended. Ants eat this honey-dew. The aphides, when in large numbers, injure young shoots and twigs. A very pretty little one is found in Kamaon on the 'dabree' tree. They excrete a white substance of a sweet taste, which cakes on the leaves. Another aphis is found on the sal or Shorea robusta.

Aphis coffeæ, the coffee louse, is found in small communities on the young shoots and on the underside of the leaves of the cocoa-nut tree, but occasions little injury.

The t'hela disease is caused by the Aphis lanigera, a viviparous wingless parasite, with a flask-shaped body, six feet, two antennæ, two tubes at abdominal extremity, a haustellum for puncturing, and a sucker for extracting, and within this transparent sucker a perfect apparatus resembling a hand-pump; the sucker is fixed, the miniature piston plays, and the sap—the life-blood of the plant—is absorbed, and its leaves are destroyed.

The oily (t'hela) honey-dew on the leaves is greedily eaten by the red and brown ants, Formica rufa and F. fusca ; and should the exudation be scanty, the ants, with their antennæ, stroke and fondle the aphis until a supply be secreted. Both sexes only exist in August, and one congress yields the young for six generations. After pairing, the female deposits eggs, which in four days animate. Immediately, from every pore in their bodies, springs a cottony substance, which covers and protects them, and they eat the leaf. As they grow, their white cover vanishes, and pale-orange wingless insects appear, the ' koongnee' of the Jats.

The Aphis lanigera does not attack cotton plants growing near hemp. They are destroyed by the lady-bird (Coccinella) and by the lace-wing (Chyrosopus).—*Ed. Rev., Oct.* 1886 ; *Moquin Tandon.*

Apidæ. A family of hymenopterous insects, popularly known as bees. The principal genera are Apis (the honey bees), Melipona, Trigona, Bombus (the humble bees), Apathus, Anthophora, Xylocopa (the carpenter bees), Englossa, Osmia, Megachile (the leaf-cutting bees), Anthocoma, Nomada, Halictus, Sphecodes. Some bees in the East are markedly revengeful and even aggressive. At the Harn Pal, on the Nerbada, bees have twice caused Europeans to be drowned. The common hive-bee of Britain is Apis mellifica ; the ' Italian bee ' is Apis ligustica; the principal honey bee of the East Indies is the Apis dorsata.

Araneidæ, the spiders, an order of the Arachnoidea class of animals, of which several thousand species are known. They are among the most powerful insect friends of man, and they contribute more perhaps than any other family to check the too rapid multiplication of insects. The families are—

Mygalidæ or crab-spiders, with the genera Mygale, Atypus, Cteniza, Actinopus, Nemesia.

Theridiidæ, genera Latrodectus and Theridion.

Lycosidæ, wolf - spiders, genera Lycosa, with other thirteen British families.

Species of the Mygalidæ and Lycosidæ are among the pests of India. Spiders are kept under by their attacks on each other ; they are at war with all small insects ; they are eaten by monkeys, squirrels, lizards, and frogs, and a genus of birds, the Arachnotheræ, the spider hunters of India and Malayana, are their natural enemies.

Arctia. A genus of moths belonging to the Bombyces. There are several species in India, one of which, Arctia Horsfieldi, attacks the cotton plant.

Argades are arachnida which are closely allied to the ticks ; they differ from them by the inferior situation of the mouth, and by their free conical palpi composed of four articulations. There are several species. Argas Persicus, *Fischer*, is common at Miana, in Persia. Its size is about that of the common bug; the body is rough, of a blood-red colour, and covered with some elevated white spots ; these parasites attack man. In Persia it is said that they give the preference to strangers (?) The bite produces acute pain, and it has been even asserted that they may bring on consumption and death. Species of argas occur in Europe, Africa, and America. —*Fischer ; M. T.*

Artaxa guttata, *Walker.* Its larva attacked a castor-oil plant, sown in England.

B

Badhya, of Hindustan. Blight attacks growing sorghum, penicillaria, and zea.

Bakoli, of Hindustan. A green caterpillar which destroys rice crops.

Bala, of Hindustan. A grub which eats the young shoots of wheat and barley when about six inches high.

Bangka, or Katua, of Hindustan. A beetle which eats the rice plant. The scientific names of these four are desiderata. Vernacular terms vary in different places.

Batocera. A genus of Longicorn coleoptera, of the family Lamiidæ. There are several species in India, varying from three to five inches in length, with long spiny horns. One of them, Batocera ruber, the curuminga beetle of Ceylon and Southern India, penetrates the trunks of young cocoa-nut trees near the ground, and deposits its eggs near the centre. The grubs, when hatched, eat their way to the top, and destroy the leaf. Sometimes a whole plantation is attacked.

Bear.—See Mammalia.

Beer Casks.—See Tomicus.

Bees. The popular name for the hymenopterous insects of the family Apidæ.—See Apidæ.

Beetles. The popular name for insects of the order Coleoptera. Beetles are very numerous, and a few of them are useful to man ; others destroy timber and seeds. A red beetle of Northern India is described in Mr. Firminger's book on gardening as very destructive to cucurbitaceous fruits. Species of Cerosterna, Euchirus, Ligurus, Lucanidæ, Melolonthidæ, are among the more destructive.—See Coleoptera.

Belostoma Indicum. A large water-bug.

Blight is a general term in husbandry, commonly applied to denote the effects of disease or other occurrence which causes plants to wither or decay.

Blister-beetles.—See Cantharidæ.

Bombyx. A species known to the natives of India as the Bhooa and Buro bhooa, has a caterpillar which feeds on the castor-oil plant and Cocculus acuminatus. The insect deposits its eggs in flimsy cocoons on the lower surface of the leaves of the castor-oil plant. Each brood contains about 300 individuals; and for a few days after the young caterpillars emerge from the eggs, they form a dense, wriggling, maggot-like swarm, each a line in length, thread-like, and of a greyish colour. These rapidly increase in size, are extremely voracious, and devour each other, at least 75 per cent. being thus destroyed. Mynas and other birds shun them. The full-grown caterpillar is from 1½ to 2 inches in length, of a dull olive-green, with dorsal and lateral stripes of a blackish-brown colour, and with fascicles of long silky hairs. The moths emerge from the cocoon in 15 or 20 days. They are of a pale buff colour. Mr. Scott supposed that the insectivorous birds avoid the caterpillar of this bombyx, from its mimicry of a smaller one also affecting the castor-oil plant, very similar in colour and shagginess, but with brittle hairs which cause intolerable itching if applied externally, and, if taken internally, give rise to dangerous and not infrequently fatal consequences. Goats and buffaloes are so affected on swallowing one or more of these caterpillars with the castor-oil leaves. The first symptoms are inflammation of the bowels, followed by excessive purging, which not infrequently ends in death.

Bombyx, *sp.*, the Tiliayakura of the natives of Hindustan, appeared in Behar in 1877–78 on the poppy plant, causing great destruction.—*J. Scott.*

Book-worm, the death-watch, a beetle which bores through the leaves and boards of books; it is a species of Anobium. Among the insects which infest books in India are two useful genera, the chelifer and the lepisma, known respectively as the tailless scorpion and the fish insect. Both of these shun the light, but they pursue and greedily feed on the larvæ of the death-watch, and the numerous acari and soft-bodied insects which prey on books. Leaves of the margosa tree are placed in books to protect them, as also the powdered leaves of Justicia gandarussa. The seeds of the Nigella sativa and camphor are placed among the books to scare insects.— See Anobium.

Borer. A popular term adopted in India to designate several different insects which bore into and destroy economic plants. A borer-worm of India, with a white flaccid body and reddish-hued head, is described as committing great havoc in gardens and shrubberies of Southern India. It attacks all manner of shrubs and trees indiscriminately, piercing the stem about two feet from the ground, and then boring downwards through the root into the earth, and effectually killing the tree or shrub. Eucalyptus, acacia, and woodbine or honeysuckle appear especially subject to its depredations.—See Batocera; Diatræa; Tomicus.

Bostrichus. A genus of the Xylophagi. The species chiefly affect the dead wood of forest trees.—*R. T.*

Bots are larvæ of insects of the family Œstridæ.—See Œstridæ.

Brarrah, of Swat. A wood-louse that infests houses in

which old mats are lying about. Their bites become red and inflamed. Its scientific name needs to be determined.

Brassica campestris, *Linn.,* sub-species B. napus, *Linn.,* the rape, is peculiarly liable to the attacks of a species of blight, and in damp seasons in the North-Western Provinces, every plant in a field is not uncommonly covered with tiny insects (aphides), which suck the sap from the flowering shoots, and effectually prevent any seed from forming.—*D. & F.—Vern. Rai.—Sarson.*

Bruchus and **Rhynchites** are weevils of the family Rhynchophora, order Coleoptera. They are small, but their ravages are of the highest detriment to the reproductiveness of the forests of the North-Western Provinces. Entire seed crops of the Shorea robusta were destroyed in the year 1863. All the weevil family insert their eggs in the stigma of the flower, which, when developed, has introduced the young larvæ (which are hatched meanwhile) into the recently formed fruit or pericarp. In this the larvæ live till nearly mature, when, by their encroachments towards the stalk, they cause the seed or fruit to fall, and they escape into the earth to undergo the transformation into the pupa state. Species of bruchus are highly destructive of the forests of Northern India. Bruchus weevils attack most leguminous seed-pods,—peas, beans, gram; and live in the seed till perfectly developed, when they escape by making an oval or circular orifice. Bruchus granarius, *Linn.,* is the bean-beetle of Europe. Two species of bruchus attack the stored poppy seed both in the larva and perfect state. One of them, about four lines long, is of a brownish colour, with its wing cases striated. It rapidly shells the seeds, which also are injured and united by the gluey nature of its excrement, the pellets becoming enveloped in a pale rose-coloured mould,—the Dactylium roseum, —which soon destroys their germinating power.

Another species of smaller size also injures the poppy seed.—*R. T.; J. Scott.*

Bug is a popular term applied to several genera of noxious insects, usually to those of two families of Hemiptera. Cimex lectularius, the bed bug, one of the Cimicidæ, belongs to the order Hemiptera and to the family Geocores; they are very troublesome in Indian houses. Notonecta glauca, of Europe, is a species of water bug, commonly known as the boat-fly. Plant bugs of the order Heteroptera, families Scutata, Coreidæ, and Phytocoridæ, live upon plants, trees, and shrubs, and feed upon the juices which they suck out of the soft tissues, many of them attacking juicy fruits. It was the bugs and the borers chiefly that ruined the coffee industry of Ceylon, with the loss to the Europeans engaged in it of millions of gold. Other insects active in the work there have been the mealy bug, Pseudococcus adonidum; a black bug, Lecanium nigrum; a moth, Agrotis segetum; the white bug, a species of Ancylonychus, one of the Coleoptera, and the brown or scaly bug, Lecanium coffeæ; but the Aphides or plant-lice, with species of the Lepidoptera or butterflies, and the moth Phymatea punctata, have aided in the ruin. In Europe, Lecanium hesperidum, one of the Coccidæ, attacks the orange, and Coccus adonidum is often mischievous in hot-houses. The stones of the Cordia myxa of the Kamaon forests are sucked by a large red bug.

A green bug of Burma, one of the Tingidæ, is very injurious to fruit. They suck the juice of oranges through the skin. The paddy bug of Burma sucks the paddy before the husk has become hard. It is a species of Cimex, or one of the Scutelleridæ, and whole fields of rice are sometimes abandoned in consequence of the devastation it commits. Some of the bugs are most attractive in colour; a green one is often seen on leaves. They are quite inoffensive if unmolested, but if irritated exhale an offensive odour. Hem Chundra Dutta of Calcutta says that if mulberry trees be grown in the coffee plantations, the coffee bug forsakes the coffee plant for the better-liked mulberry leaf.—*R. T.*—See Cimicidæ.

Bunka, of Hindustan. A hairy caterpillar that eats the leaves of the cotton plant; it has not been identified.

Buprestis is a genus of insects of the order Coleoptera, family Serricornes. The larvæ are very destructive to living and dead vegetable substances. The Buprestidæ are peculiarly forest insects, and in Northern India attack the timber of coniferous trees.

A small species of Buprestis, along with a Cerambyx, attacks the wood of the Shorea robusta, in the forests of Kamaon and Garhwal. The grubs of the Buprestidæ family exist in timber for a number of years before turning out the perfect insect. After acquiring maturity, they bore into the timber to the depth of two or three inches, and then undergo their metamorphosis. These beetles often render timber unfit for use. They commence underneath the bark. The larvæ of a species of Buprestis was found by Mr. R. Thompson boring two or three inches into felled logs of sal (Shorea robusta), in the Kotree Doon. He found another Buprestis in the dead timber of a living acacia catechu tree, and another in the trunk of a living mango tree. A small Buprestis of a shining colour is frequently found in the timber of the Cheer pine, Pinus longifolia, quite destroying the logs

It is only in the bark that the females can deposit their eggs, the sapwood and newly-formed bark affording the larva nourishment; and to protect felled timber, the bark should be removed as soon as the tree is felled.—*R. T.*— See Coleoptera.

Burying-beetles.—See Coleoptera; Silphidæ.

Buthus afer.—See Scorpion.

Butterflies are said to be 10,000 or 12,000 in number. Few of them have an economic value, and many of their caterpillars are very destructive to the leaves of vegetables. Some butterflies have a wide range.   Danais chrysippus butterfly extends from Greece to the East Indies.   It is mimicked by Elymnias undularis, Argynnis niphe and A. inconstans, Hypolimnas misippus, Euphœdra eleus, Papilio merope, and Charyatis phileta.   Others are objects of wonder.   Kallima inachis is the leaf butterfly of India, and K. paralekta, of Sumatra, resembles dead leaves.

C

Cajanus Indicus, *Sprenger*, the pigeon-pea, has its principal enemy in frost; in the North-Western Provinces a single cold night utterly ruins the crops of a whole district.— *D. & F.—Vern. Arhar, Dāl.*

Calandra.   A genus of insects belonging to the order Coleoptera, family Rhynchophora.   Some of the calandra group are particularly destructive to grain, pulse, and millet; others attack the sugar-cane and the palmyra tree. Several of the species of calandra are popularly known as weevils.   C. granaria is the grain weevil; C. oryzæ is the rice weevil, which destroys rice, maize, and other food-grains; C. palmarum injures the palmyra tree; C sacchari injures the sugar-cane. C. comuta is the common maize weevil of Bengal.—*J. Scott.*—See Coleoptera ; Curculionidæ.

Cannabis sativa, *Linn.*, the hemp plant, is grown throughout all the south of Asia ; that of the North-Western Provinces is by the lowest class of cultivators, and the phrase, ' May hemp be sown in thy house,' is one of the commonest abusive imprecations. Its several products, charras, bhang, sabza or siddhi, ganja, are hurtful intoxicants. They are indulged in by the men of several of the races of India, and insanity has often been traced to their use. Women are not addicted to their use. A person intoxicated with charras is often unconscious for a day or two.—*D. & F.*

Cantharidæ. A family of insects with irritating properties. The blistering flies of India are chiefly the Mylabris or Meloe cichorii, the Cantharis gigas, and the Cantharis violacea. Mylabris cichorii is common in the neighbourhood of Dacca, in the Hyderabad country, in Kurnool, and numerous other localities. Dr. Hunter published a good account of this in the fifth vol. of the *Transactions of the Asiatic Society,* p. 216. The insect is about an inch long, and one-third broad; the elytra or wing coverts are marked with six cross stripes of deep blue and russet brown. The Cantharis violacea is often mixed with specimens of meloe in the bazaars. The Telini fly, if procured before the mites have commenced its destruction, yields on an average one-third more of cantharidin than the Spanish fly of the European shops. The blue fly is of uncertain strength ; Meloe trianthema is so called from its being usually found on the plant named Trianthema decandra (biscopra, Hind.). The Indian blistering beetles, Mylabris pustulata and M. punctum, are found in large quantities at certain seasons all over Southern India. M. cichorii and M. pustulata are used by the Chinese.

Meloe is a name given to a genus of insects allied to Mylabris and Cantharis; they are remarkable for the shortness of the elytra and the absence of wings. When the larvæ are born they attach themselves to hymenoptera, which are searching for food; by this means they are transported to the nests of the bees, where they continue to live and complete their development. When a meloe is irritated or attempted to be captured, it discharges from the joints of the legs a viscid acrid liquid, of a yellow colour, and having the odour of amber or of violets.

'The vesicating insects possess a singular softness of the elytra and the integument, differing from that of other insect tribes. The explanation of this fact is found in the histological, and not on the chemical, characters of the wing, as was at one time supposed. Between the two layers, which are connected at their edges by chitin, there is a considerable space, and the two layers are connected by chitinous pillars, which, although thin and delicate, form substantial supports. In most other insects the chitinous layers are much thicker, the pillars more numerous, and the spaces are almost obliterated. The peculiarities noted have, it is believed, much to do with the irritating nature produced by minute particles of wings when applied to the skin of human beings.'

Capnodium mangiferum inflicts injury on the trees it inhabits similar to that of the coffee-rot. It obstructs the stomata of the leaf to which it adheres. The Artocarpus integrifolia, Ficus asperrimum, Mangifera Indica, Sponia Wightii, are their favourite trees.

Carthamus tinctorius, *Linn.*, plants are reported to

suffer occasionally from an insect known as the 'al.' The people imagine that if there be lightning while the heads are in flower, great injury is occasioned. This is sown, intermixed with other seeds, to keep off deer, as they dread its prickly leaves.—*D. & F.*—*Vern. Kusum.*

Cassida, *sp.,* the tortoise beetle, attacks the artichoke.— *R. T.*

Caterpillars. The caterpillars of Orgyia Ceylanica, Euproctis virguncula, Trichia exigua, Narosa conspersa, Limacodes graciosa, and a species of Drepana, do not cause much injury to coffee. One caterpillar, however, the Zeuzera coffeæ, destroys many trees, both young and old, by eating out the heart. It resembles the caterpillar of the great moth of England, and is as thick as a goose quill. It generally enters the tree 6 to 12 inches from the ground, and makes its way upwards. The sickly drooping of the tree marks its presence. Caterpillars of the Boarmia leucostigmaria and B. Ceylanica, also those of Eupithecia coffearia, are found on coffee and other trees in Ceylon from September to December. Some Ceylon caterpillars sting; one of them—short, broad, and pale-green, with fleshy spines, that feeds on the Carissa jasminiflora, and stings with fury—is of the moth Ncœra lepida, *Cramer* (the Limacodes graciosa, *West.*). The larvæ of the genus Adolia are hairy, and sting with virulence. That of an undetermined species of moth of Bengal causes great damage, its broods successively appearing with every young crop. They are preyed upon by the crows and mynas. Another undefined caterpillar, when young of a uniformly pale-green colour, infests the poppy plant in its later stages, and feeds alike on the leaves and maturing seeds. It gradually acquires a yellowish-brown tinge, and finally a dull grey, with two lateral brown stripes.

It attacks only the exhausted capsules, and destroys the seed.   They are kept under by the pied starling, or ' ablaq myna,' the Sturnopastor contra of naturalists.

A small white round worm, in the Vizagapatam district, is found at the root of young graft mango trees, which they kill.   Their presence is detected by a loosening of the earth around the root-stem, and the presence of small ants of a grey colour, covering the ground.   It, too, awaits identification.

Many caterpillars exactly resemble in tint the leaves they feed upon, others are like little brown twigs, and many are so strangely marked or humped, that when motionless they can hardly be taken to be living creatures at all.—*J. Scott ; Tennent's Ceylon.*—See Butterflies.

Cecidomyia oryzæ, *Wood - Mason.*   About the year 1879–80, an insect in Monghir threatened to become very destructive to the rice crops.   Mr. Wood-Mason identified it as belonging to the genus Cecidomyia, and as related to the Hessian fly which ravaged the wheat fields in the United States.   This genus, Mr. Wood-Mason says, had never before been found in India, and he proposed to call the species Cecidomyia oryzæ, or the rice-fly. He considered it as likely to prove a most formidable pest, and recommended that the district officers should be instructed to make further inquiries, and carefully watch its progress.

Cecidomyia tritici and **Lasioptera** obfuscata are wheat midges.   The former is the Hessian fly of Europe and America, and the latter is of Great Britain.   Those of India await attention.— *W.-M.*

Cerambyx vatica, *R. Thompson,* has been so named by Mr. Thompson because of its peculiarly attacking the wood of the sal tree, Shorea robusta : not, however, in its healthy and vigorous state; but no sooner has the flow of healthy sap ceased, than a host of young larvæ of the Cerambyx vatica are hatched. This species never attacks the timber when the bark has been removed; and it is only after the tree has been killed and the bark allowed to remain that it is resorted to by the beetles for the purpose of breeding. This and a little buprestis are the only beetles that attack sal wood in the forests of Kamaon and Garhwal.—*R. Thompson.*

Cerambyx, *sp.* In some localities of Kamaon and Garhwal, however, the larvæ of a species of Cerambyx attack the young saplings in the sal forests to a very great extent. Like the grub of the Prionus on the tea plant, this Cerambyx first bores downwards, then up, destroying the pith, and eating for itself a round channel, extending from the root to the highest point that the insect can reach without disclosing the place of its retreat. The plant is killed. Trees affected by this insect may, however, be known by the little heaps of sawdust-looking excrement collected at their roots, ejected through an aperture made on purpose by the insect.

Cerambyx, *sp.* The Cedrela toona and Dalbergia sissoo trees are both affected by a larger species of Cerambyx than is found on sal. Also, a minute species attacks the living bark of Acacia catechu. They get underneath the bark, and eat away the newly-formed wood. Their presence within the tree is detected by the exudation of a gummy substance.—*R. Thompson.*

Cerambyx, *sp.* The larva of another species attacks the Rottlera tinctoria. This is over four lines long, and as thick as the thumb.

The grubs of a species inhabit the mango and pine trees.

Cerastes. A genus of horned serpents, allied to the

vipers.   The principal species are the Cerastes Ægyptiacus
and Cerastes Persicus.—*M. T.*—See Snakes.

Ceriosterna gladiator, a longicorn beetle, which eats
away the bark and destroys the leading shoot of the
casuarina tree.   Valuable casuarina plantations have
been successfully formed along the shore of the Coromandel
coast, but they have a nocturnal enemy in this Ceriosterna
gladiator.

Chelifer, *sp.*, tailless scorpions, are not injurious though
so supposed.   They live on mites and wood-lice, eating up
these insect pests of books.   There are several species
widely distributed.—See Anobium.

Chrysomelidæ larvæ attack the cotton plant.

Cicadella, *sp.*, attack the cotton plant.

Cicadidæ.   A family of the order Rhynchota and sub-
order Homoptera.   Tacua speciosa is a black species of the
Eastern Archipelago.   In the China tea-boxes is another
black species with yellow spots (Gæana maculata), and a
smaller black species with blood-red abdomen (Huechys
sanguinea).   The Cicadidæ live upon trees and shrubs,
sucking out the juices of the young tender shoots and roots.

Cicendela Chinensis.   A richly-coloured species of the
tiger-beetles, is abundant in the rice fields of China and
Japan.   C. octoguttata of Assam is an inch in length.

Cicer arietinum, *Linn.*, suffers greatly from frost, if
caught by it in flower, and whole fields of healthy plants
are sometimes ruined by a cold night in January or
February.   Great injury also often results from the
ravages of the ' bahādura ' caterpillar.   It awaits identification.—*D. & F.*—*Vern. Chana.*

Cimicidæ, or bugs, belong to the order Hemiptera and
to the family Geocores.   Helopeltis Antonii is a name of
the tea-bug.—*M. T.*—See Bug ; Tea-bug.

Clothes Moths.—See Tineidæ.

Coccidæ. A family of Homopterous insects known as scale-insects.—See Coccus.

Coccinella are known as the lady-bird or lady-cow. In the larval and mature stages they are said to feed exclusively on the injurious parasites on plants of the aphides or plant-lice; but, in Bengal, a twelve-spotted species undoubtedly feeds on the leaves and flower-buds of nearly all the Cucurbitaceæ.—*J. Scott.*—See Coleoptera.

Coccus adonidum, in the hot-houses of Europe, often commits great injury.—See Lecanium; Pseudococcus.

Cockroach. This name is given to the Periplaneta orientalis, and the American P. americana. Also to species of the genera Blatta, Blabera, Panchlora, Phoraspis. They destroy the young shoots and flower stem of orchids. They soil and injure books and clothes, and are peculiarly troublesome in ships. They shun the light.

Cocoa-nut palm. Cocoa-nut trees have great enemies in the shape of two beetles. One of these is a large Curculio (Rhynchophorus, *Sach.*), called the red beetle, nearly as big as the stag-beetle of Britain; the other is the Oryctes rhinoceros, so called from its projecting horn. The red beetle is so called from the red mark on the upper part of its breast. Its attacks are said to be on the nut, but those of the rhinoceros beetle are on the terminal bud of the palm stem. When so injured, the bud dies, and, the crown of the leaves falling off, leaves the cocoa-nut tree a mere bare stem. The same result occurs to other palms, as the palmyra, the betel, etc., in which the top bud, or cabbage as it is called, is destroyed.

Coffee trees have been injured by many insects and plants. Mr. R. C. Haldane, in 1881, in his book, '*All about*

Grubs,' gave the Singhalese vernacular names and figures of several pests, and of these Mr. Ch. O. Waterhouse has identified the Aræocerus coffeæ, Anomola elata, Camarimena variabile, Clinteria chloronata, Lachnosterna pinguis, Leucopholis pinguis, and Mimela xanthorrhina.

Mr. Nietner, in 1860, gave the following list of the enemies of the coffee trees in Ceylon, viz.—

Coleoptera.

Pseudococcus adonidum, white or mealy bug.
Lecanium coffeæ, *Walk. List. Ins. B. M.*, brown or scaly bug.
L. nigrum, *N.*, black bug.
Syncladium Nietneri, *Rabh. Dresd. Hedwig,* 1858; Trisposporium
    Gardneri, *Berk. J. Hort. Soc. Lond.,* 1849.
Aphis coffeæ, *N.*, coffee louse.
Strachia geometrica, *Motch. in lits.*

Lepidoptera.

Aloa lactinea, *Cram., pap. ex.*
Orgyia Ceylanica, *N.*
Euproctis virguncula, *Walk.*
Trichia exigua, *Feld. in. lit.*
Narosa conspersa, *Walk.*
Limacodes graciosa, *Westw., Ent. cat.*
Drepana ?
Zeuzera coffeæ, *N.*
Agrotis segetum, *Wien. V.*, black grub.
Galleriomorpha lichenoides, *Feld. in lit.*
Boarmia Ceylanica, *Feld. in lit.*
B. leucostigmaria, *Feld. in lit.*
Eupithecia coffearia, *Feld. in lit.*
Tortrix coffearia, *Feld. in lit.*
Gracillaria ? coffeifoliella, *Motch.*

Diptera.

Anthomyza ? coffeæ, *N. in Motch.*

Orthoptera.

Phymatea punctata, *D.*
Ancylonicha, *sp. ?* white grub.
Arhines ? destructor, *N.*

Aptera.

Acarus coffeæ, *N.*

Mammalia.

Golunda Ellioti, *Gray in Kel. Prod.*, coffee rat.

A most destructive fungus, the Hemileia vastatrix, appeared in 1871, and completed the ruin of the Ceylon coffee industry, reducing the yield one-half.

Coffee-borer is a name applied to several beetles, especially to a small longicorn (Xylotrechus quadripes), which causes terrible damage to young trees ; the larvæ boring into all parts of the trees.—See Borer.

Cold Season. Insects affecting the cold season crops are species of Aphis, Cassida, Coccinella, Haltica, Locusta, and Thyca eucharis.—*R. T.*

Coleoptera is the order of insects commonly known as beetles. Some 90,000 species have already been described, and some thousands of new ones are annually being discovered. The principal families are :—

The Cicendelidæ and Carabidæ (tiger beetles and ground beetles). Nearly all of these are beneficial, and are carnivorous. Dyticidæ, water-beetles, also carnivorous. Staphylinidæ, mostly carnivorous. Silphidæ, the burying beetles. The species of Necrophorus and Silpha are useful ; they feed on carrion, and by scratching the ground from under dead animals, they partially bury them (whence their name).

Dermestidæ. The species of this family feed chiefly on dry animal matter. The larvæ of Dermestes are about half an inch long, clothed with long erect hair, most of them being brown in colour. They do much mischief to skins.

Dermestes vulpinus is found in most parts of the world. Dermestes lardarius is the bacon-beetle. The larvæ of anthrenus are similar to those of dermestes, but much smaller, and have tufts of stiff hair at their tails, which they erect when alarmed.

Anthrenus museorum does much mischief in museums.

Anthrenus vorax did much damage to the stores of soldiers' coats in India.

Scarabæidæ. Nearly all the species live in dung, including the sacred-beetle (Scarabæus sacer). Some species of this family in India are of great size (Heliocopris midas), measuring more than two inches in length. The Melolonthidæ (cockchafers) and the Rutelidæ, both feed on living vegetable matter, chiefly on roots of grasses, shrubs, and trees, often doing much mischief. Leucopholis pinguis, Lachnosterna pinguis, Mimela xanthorrhina, Anomala elata cause much damage to coffee trees. The Cetoniidæ (the rose-beetles), very similar in their habits to the Melolonthidæ; one species, Clinteria chloronata, does much mischief to coffee trees, the grub eating the roots, and the beetle the blossoms.

Buprestidæ and Elateridæ (click-beetles); the larvæ feed on living wood, and are more or less injurious.

Tenebrionidæ, a large family, few of which are injurious; Tenebrio is the meal-worm beetle.

Cantharidæ, the blister-beetles.

Curculionidæ, the weevils, including Calandra and Rhynchophorus, the palm weevils; Sitophilus orizæ and granarius, the corn weevils. Bruchidæ, very destructive to seeds, especially beans.

Anthribidæ. One species of this group (Aræocerus coffeæ) does much mischief to seeds of various kinds, including coffee beans, and is met with nearly all over the world.

Prionidæ, Cerambycidæ, and Lamiidæ, the long-horned beetles. The larvæ of these beetles live on both living and dead wood, and often do much mischief. Some of the beetles themselves also injure the trees by gnawing off the smaller twigs.

Chrysomelidæ. The larvæ of these insects are chiefly injurious to the leaves of plants.

Coccinellidæ. 'Lady-birds or cow-ladies.' These are beneficial in the larval and perfect state, both feeding voraciously on the Aphidæ or blight. A species, however, in Bengal, with twelve spots, undoubtedly feeds on the leaves and flower-buds of nearly all the Cucurbitaceæ.

The insects of Northern India most destructive to living and dead vegetable substances belong to five families of Coleoptera, to two families of the Hemiptera or bugs, to one of the Neuroptera or lace wings, and to three of the Hymenoptera.

The forest trees of Northern India suffer largely from the genera Bostrichus, Bruchus, Buprestis, Calandra, Cerambyx, Curculio, Euchirus, Hylesinus, Lamia, Leptura, Lucanus, Monochamus, Prionus, Rhyncoenus, Saperda, Scolytus, Tomicus. These belong to five families, viz. Lamellicornes, Longicornes, Rhynchophora, Serricornes, and Xylophagi.

The larvæ of the family Buprestidæ, species of the Lucanus, stag-beetles; species of Euchirus; species of the wood boring Xylophagi, Bostrichus, Tomicus, and Hylesinus, are all of them very destructive. The Buprestidæ are peculiarly forest insects, attacking the timber of coniferous trees of Northern India. The Lucanidæ, stag-beetles, are pre-eminently wood feeders. They live in their larva stage in the interior of the trunks of large trees. A very large proportion of the species of Coleoptera do not come forth of their hiding places until dusk, and a large number even pass their whole lives in concealment.

Coreidæ.—See Cicadidæ.

Corn-weevil.—See Coleoptera; Curculionidæ.

Cotton.—See Gossypium.

Crickets, house, field, and mole, belong to the order Orthoptera, and family Gryllidæ.—See Cylindrodes ; Gryllidæ ; Schizodactylus.

Crocodiles are numerous in the rivers of Africa and Southern and Eastern Asia, and are of two families, Crocodilidæ and Gavialidæ; another family, the Alligatoridæ, are reptiles of America. Crocodiles evince great cunning, and carry off many people, both young and old, and devour innumerable fish. Man does not escape ; and people in boats, as also goats, dogs, and ponies venturing near the river-sides, are seized by their great jaws, or are swept into the water by their tail. There has not been adopted any systematic mode of destroying them, yet it would not be difficult to discover their nests and destroy their eggs. Their nests rise two feet out of the water, and the Rev. Bancroft Boake mentions that Mr. Symonds in Ceylon found 150 eggs in one nest. A net of strong rope with a hook is used to catch them.

Crotalaria juncea, *Linn.*, the san hemp, is sometimes used to clean land, as the closeness of its growth stifles all weeds which may attempt to compete with it.—*D. & F.*—*Vern. San.*

Culex is a genus of the Culicidæ, gnats and mosquitos, both of them painfully harassing to man and animals. Mosquito, gnat, midge are popular names applied to different insects of the family Culicidæ. The females only are greedy of blood ; if this fail them, they live like the males on the juices of flowers. The females alone pierce the skin, by means of an auger with teeth at the end ; they suck the blood, and, before they fly away, distil a liquid venom into the wound. The bite seems to have an anæsthetic effect, which does not cause it to be felt till some time after. And if the mosquito be killed before it has injected the poison into the wound, there is no subsequent pain or irritation.

Mosquitos, in the Tumiche creek in the Gunnison Valley, Colorado, when the small young trout rise to the surface to breathe, will alight on the trout's head and kill it. (*Sc. Gos.*, Nov. 1885.) The larvæ of the dragon flies destroy young fish. In the damp parts of India, mosquitos abound. At eventide they rise in myriads from the Irawadi, and cling around the trees like clouds, and the poorest Burman sleeps under a mosquito curtain. If the itching sensation which their bites occasion be yielded to and the part be scratched, numerous and sometimes large leg sores are formed. The *Edinburgh Review* for October 1886 mentions that ' rich and fertile portions of the Southern United States are incapable of cultivation from the hosts of mosquitos that abound in them. The same insect effectually shuts out portions of British America from exploration.' In India, the people, to scare away mosquitos, suspend a plant of the Aloe perfoliata; the Chinese burn wormwood rolled up in the form of pastilles with some fragrant resin. Pennyroyal plants suspended in a room are said to be equally effective against fleas, flies, and mosquitos.—*Van Beneden*, 116.

Curculionidæ are weevils. They attack, principally in their larva stage, every part of vegetable tissues, and all sorts of plant life. These larvæ are very destructive alike to forests and orchards, and to seeds and cereals stored in granaries. A large number of the Curculionidæ pass the early stages of their metamorphosis in the pith of stems of trees and plants.—See Coleoptera

Cylindrodes Campbelli, a mole-cricket, one of the Gryllidæ, inhabits Melville Island, on the north coast of Australia; is about 2½ inches long. It burrows into the stems of plants, and causes them to wither.—See Cricket; Gryllidæ.

Cynips. The gall-producing insects are numerous and of great variety in the forests of the North-Western Provinces. They puncture and lay their eggs in large numbers in the fruits, seeds, and leaves of plants, and the excrescences are known as galls. Cynips of the common gall is the Cynips gallæ tinctoria, *Linn.* Another species is C. quercus folii, *Linn.*, and a third is the C. quercus tojæ, *Fabr.*—*R. T.*—See Galls.

D

Deiopeia pulchella is widely distributed, and occurs in India. Its caterpillars feed on the kernel of the seed of the Phyrostigma venenosum, which contains the poisonous principle Cærenia, and its pupæ have been found entrapped in the centre of the hard bean. The excrement of its larvæ contains the principle of the bean unaltered.

Delphax saccharivora, the cane spittle-fly of Grenada and British Honduras, ravages the sugar-cane there. It has not been observed in India.

Depressaria gossipiella attacks the cotton plant of India.—See Cotton; Gossypium.

Dermestes.—See Coleoptera.

Diatræa sacchari. In the Mauritius, sugar-cane is injured by the Proceras sacchariphagus, which Mr. J. O. Westwood has supposed may be identical with the Diatræa sacchari, *Guilding,* and Phalæna saccharalis or

Chilo saccharalis, *Fabricius.* The borer of the Queensland cane has been supposed to be the larva of this Diatræa sacchari. It enters the cane on its appearing above ground, and eats up the heart. It is supposed to be identical with the borer of the Mauritius, Proceras sacchariphagus. Diatræa sacchari is the Chilo saccharalis, *Fabricius.* It occurs in the United States. The Mauritius sugar-cane is one of the varieties now cultivated in the North-Western Provinces of India, but it is not known if the Diatræa has accompanied it.

Distoma hepaticum (Fasciola hepatica), *Linn.*, the liver-fluke, is found in France, and is not uncommon in Holland, Sweden, Norway, and even in Greenland. The liver-fluke is from $\frac{8}{10}$ to $\frac{11}{10}$ of an inch in length. It causes great loss of sheep and cattle. Fasciola trachealis inhabits the windpipe of birds.—*M. T.*—See Amphistoma.

Dorcus titan, a large stag-beetle of Java, family Lucanidæ.

Doryphora. Potato beetle, the Doryphora decemlineatum, does not occur in India. The common fire-fly or lightning bug, Photinus pyralis, has been often mistaken for it.

Drepanognathus saltator, *Jerdon* (or Harpegnathus saltator, *Jerdon*), an ant of the Peninsula of India, of Malabar, and Mysore, has the name saltator from its making surprising jumps when alarmed or disturbed. It is very pugnacious, and bites and stings very severely.

Dry-rot, a disease affecting timber, is produced by the attacks of several fungi. It increases in rapidity according to the amount of potassium and phosphoric acid which is contained in the wood where it occurs. Wood felled in the spring is rich in both these materials, and dry-rot spores are easily cultivated in it; but winter-felled trees contain much less both of the acid and the potassium. Nine-tenths of the decay of timber is due to rot occasioned by the common wood fungus. This parasite develops under two conditions, namely, moisture and heat, and both are present in new, green, or unseasoned timber employed in buildings. In old or seasoned timber, the former is wanting, and hence greater durability. If moisture only be present without heat, the fungus will not grow; if heat without moisture, it equally has no scope for development, and hence the protecting influence cf ventilation.—See Fungi.

Durkhi, an insect of Hindustan, very destructive to the rice plant; it awaits identification. An insect of similar name is very destructive to the young indigo plant.

E

Elateridæ, or click - beetles, in their larva stage, are known in Britain as wire-worm. Many of the species attack all sorts of cultivated vegetable produce. In Bengal they are destructive of wheat, barley, and millets, injuring the plant, root and stalk. The larvæ of one species penetrate the potato tubers and destroy their inner parts. Wheat and barley crops, when freely mixed with mustard plants, suffer less than other crops. Some of the species live for two or three years in the larva state, and do in this time great damage to crops of corn. Larvæ of a click-beetle have been found at the roots of the Queensland sugar-cane, but no damage from them has been detected.—*J. Scott.*

Eleusine coracana, *Gærtner,* suffers greatly from heavy rain, and a good year for rice is a bad year for eleusine, and *vice versa.* It is the most profitable of the minor millets.. It can be preserved for sixty years in pits, and greatly advantages in dearths.—*Vern. Marwa.—D. & F.*

Endioptis Indica attacks the cotton plant. — See Gossypium.

Epeira, *sp.*, a large red-and-black spider, about Monghir on the Ganges, forms gigantic webs, stretching across the paths, sufficiently strong to offer considerable opposition to a traveller. The reticulated parts of the webs are of a bright yellow colour, and about 5 feet in diameter, but have a stretch of 10 to 20 feet, including the great guy ropes, by which it is fastened to some neighbouring tree or clump of bamboos. The spider sits in the centre waiting for its prey. One of them when expanded measured 6 inches across the legs. Captain Sherwill found a species of Nectarinia entangled in one of their webs.

Erythrina Indica, or dadap. A letter published in the *Weekly Ceylon Observer* for 27th November 1884 stated that the coffee‑leaf disease, Hemileia vastatrix, was caused by planting 'dadap' trees between the coffee plants for shade, and that wherever coffee is planted on forest land, or where no 'dadap' trees are used for shade, there is no sign of leaf disease. But there has not been observed in Southern India any connection between the presence of erythrina trees and the production of leaf disease; on the contrary, the effect of planting erythrina has been distinctly beneficial, not hurtful, to the coffee trees which it is planted to shade.

Eucheirus longimanus, a chafer that attacks the palms. It is known in the Moluccas as the grand sagueir feeding beetles, because they perish in thousands during the night, by dropping into the palm wine collecting buckets. It is one of the Lamellicorn Coleoptera.

Eye-Fly, a minute winged insect which appears in spring-time in myriads over all India, and clusters in doors on any hanging strip of cloth or bit of thread. They irritate the eyelids, and are popularly surmised to cause ophthalmia. They are easily destroyed by burning a cone-shaped paper.—See Pipsa.

F

Filaria, a genus of the Helmintha, *q.v.* The species are all baneful. Filaria medinensis or guinea-worm is the dracunculus. Having gained an entrance into the human body, it takes from two months to a year or more to become developed. It can be withdrawn in a few minutes from the more exposed parts of the body, by cutting down on it and inserting a probe beneath. If it be broken, inflammation and suppuration follow, of a severe form. Filaria sanguinis hominis — Dr. T. R. Lewis, M.B., Assistant Surgeon, Her Majesty's British Forces, attached to the Sanitary Commission with the Government of India, discovered this hæmatozoon as inhabiting human blood of Europeans in India. (*Report* 1871, *Sanitary Commission.*) Filariæ abound in the soft parts of many birds. Dr. Spencer Cobbold, an able writer on Entozoa, found the Filaria attenuata worm in a kite.—See Guinea-worm ; Helmintha.

Fish. Sharks, although best known to landsmen as giving cause for sorrow by their destruction of human life, are not the only dangerous inhabitants of tropical seas. Some fish are injurious when taken as food, and produce symptoms resembling those of poisoning. The deleterious effects which are produced by the tunny,

Thynnus vulgaris, *Cuv.*, after its flesh has begun to change, is well known. In Europe the barbel is very injurious at the period of reproduction. The most dangerous species belong to the genera Meletta, Sphyræna, Caranx, Scarus, and Diodon. Most of the so-termed poisonous fishes are only so at times; that is to say, when they have fed upon certain animals, at the period of reproduction, or under certain other peculiar circumstances. Such are the file fish, the conger eel, the mackerel, and the herring.

The natives of India attribute poisonous qualities to the Batrachus grunniens, rejecting them even as manure.

Meletta venenosa. During Mr. Lewis' residence at Bencoolen in 1822, great numbers of what were supposed to be Clupeonia perforata presented the unusual appearance of having red eyes. Many natives, after having eaten these fishes, were suddenly attacked with violent vomiting, which, in cases where remedies were not immediately applied, was known within an hour to terminate fatally. At the same time, such of these fishes with the ordinary silvery eyes were as formerly eaten with impunity.

This phenomenon recurred at Bencoolen during the seasons of 1823 and 1825, but not of 1824. It was surmised that the poisonous fishes had fed on a gelatinous substance which at that season exudes from the beautifully coloured coral reefs on that part of the coast of Sumatra. It is, however, more probable that the poisonous fishes were shoals of Meletta venenosa, an inhabitant of the Seychelles and the neighbouring seas, which happened in those seasons to visit Sumatra. M. Valenciennes describes this fish as being poisonous, and producing effects as noted above. (*Dr. Cantor*, p. 295.)

Colonel Playfair (*Fishes of Zanzibar*, 1866) denies these fish being poisonous.

In the Straits of Malacca, Clupeonia perforata has never been known to produce bad effects.

Species of the genus Ostracion are at times deleterious, and always so are the Meletta venenosa, and M. thryssa, *Val.*, the Caranx fallax, *Cuv.*, the Scarus capitaneus, *Cuv.*, and the Diodon tigrinus, *Cuv.* The Balistes are very indigestible, even poisonous, after they feed on certain zoophytes.

Some carps in the Himalayas, as Orcinus, are very unwholesome, or cause poisonous symptoms until accustomed to them. With strangers they set up intense colic pains, and often diarrhœa and vomiting. The Semiplotus of the Assam rivers gives rise to these symptoms with most strangers.

Dr. A. Collas, of the French Navy, writing from Pondicherry in 1861, mentioned that dangerous symptoms were produced in that community by using the *calououlouve*, which he identified as the Gobius criniger, *Cuv. et Val.* This fish is apt to affect all strangers. The people had always to remove carefully the head and intestines, and wash with repeated waters; fowls died and dogs vomited and died on eating the heads and viscera.

Some Mauritius fish are said to be unhealthy when the coral is in bloom.

Mr. Forbes mentions, in his *Eastern Archipelago*, that a species of Scarus of the lagoons of the Cocos Keeling island requires to be prepared for the table with very great care; for should the gall-bladder be ruptured, and its contents escape into the body-cavity, the flesh of the fish becomes quite poisoned. Several fatal cases had occurred in the settlement, especially among children, who, almost immediately after partaking of the flesh, were seized with giddiness and stupor, followed by death.

The siluroids Plotosus anguillaris and P. albilabris occur in the seas of the Malay Peninsula. At Penang, the latter species is less numerous than the former; both are eaten by the poorer class of natives. The wounds from both are equally dreaded. The siluroids or sheat fishes are generally well armed. They have mostly strong dorsal and pectoral spines, often serrated, with which they can inflict dangerous lacerated wounds. The siluroid Thalassophryne has a distinct poison gland. In the marine and estuary species the spinal armature is invariably present, and the serrated spines on the tails of the skates cause lacerated wounds; while the Synanceïa verrucosa has a tube at each of its dorsal spines, and a poison gland at its base. The wounds are very venomous. It is, however, rare along the coasts of India.

The spine in the tail of the Trygon uarnak inflicts a lacerated wound, and Dr. Day had to amputate the arm of a person wounded by this fish. He thinks that there may be some noxious secretion likewise occasioning irritation, as seen from the scorpion fish Saccobranchus fossilis and the Clarias magur. Indian natives believe that the Saccobranchus fossilis and Clarias give poisonous wounds, but no glands have as yet been detected in them. Yet should a native be wounded in the hand, most acute inflammation at once sets in. In one instance the arm up to the shoulder, in a few hours, enlarged to double its normal size, accompanied by intense agony.

Punctured wounds, in which no direct poison has been traced, are especially dreaded from species of Pterois and their allies. The spines about the head of Platycephalus, and the spine at the side of the tail in the lancet fish Acanthurus, give more a flesh than a punctured wound. With wounds from simple spines, the symptoms seem to be mostly due to the state of health of the recipient. Species of Polyacanthus inflict punctured wounds with the spinous rays of their dorsal fins.

Species of Tetrodon have the power of inflating the abdomen, and in this state, when taken or handled, they emit a grating sound. They are also remarkable for tenacity of life, which they are capable of sustaining for several hours after having been taken out of their element. They have a peculiar, disagreeable, odour, resembling that of the Gobioidæ, which continues for several years in specimens preserved in spirits of wine. Some species of Tetrodon are undoubtedly poisonous, and one species is used in Japan for committing suicide. In the Malayan countries they are considered poisonous, and are even objected to as manure.

Teuthis, *Linn.* All the species of this genus are edible, though supposed by the Malays of the Straits to be highly poisonous. They are not eaten by them, but set aside among offal of fish to be used as manure.— *Cuvier and Valenciennes; F. D.; M. T.*

Flea.—See Pulex.

Flies. — May-flies are species of the Ephemeridæ. Dragon-flies belong to the Libellulidæ. The larvæ of certain flies often torment the human species.

The flesh-fly is the Sarcophaga carnaria, *Meig.*, Musca carnaria, *Linn.* Its body is of a golden-yellow anteriorly, and covered with long, stout, black hairs. The blue-fly or meat-fly is the Calliphora vomitoria, *Rob. Desv.*, Musca vomitoria, *Linn.*, M. chrysocephala, *De Geer;* it makes a loud buzzing noise. The golden-fly is the Lucilia Cæsar,

Rob. Desv., Musca Cæsar, *Linn.* The hominivorous fly, L. hominivora, inhabits Cayenne. The larvæ of the Musca meteorica, *Fabr.*, is sometimes developed in the stomach of man. The blue-bottle and some other flies give birth to larvæ already hatched : the blue-bottle to 200,000, which in 24 hours will increase two hundred times in weight, and eat up refuse animal matters. Linnæus said that three individuals of M. vomitoria will devour a dead horse as quickly as a lion could do it.—*M. T. ; Phipson.* —See Muscidæ.

Fluke.—See Distoma.

Flying Fox is the name given by Europeans in India to frugivorous bats of the family Pteropodidæ, genera Pteropus and Cynopterus. They roost during the day on trees, generally in large colonies, to the number of many hundreds, often, occupying a single tree. Towards sunset they fly off, sometimes to great distances, to trees that are in fruit, for the garden fruits, and those of the nim, ber, and fig trees, returning at early dawn from their hunting - grounds to their roosting tree, where they wrangle to get the best places, striking with their wing claw, screaming and cackling, and circling round the tree till they can hook on. They hang with their heads down. The Galeopithecus volans, or flying lemur, and the flying squirrels, species of Pteromys, are similarly raiders on fruit gardens.—*J.*

Frog.—See Reptile.

Fungi of various genera are cause of detriment to valuable vegetable products, and animals even do not escape. Among the more hurtful in India are species of Capundium, Chætomium, Clasterisporum, Diplodia, Dothidea, Eurotium, Glenospora, Hemileia vastatrix, Hendersonia, Hydnum, Isaria, Lentinus, Pellicularia,

Pestalozzia, Puccinia, Russula, Septoria, Uromyces, and Ustilago.

Some fungi are important as food, while others are poisonous, or are destructive to the plants upon which they grow, and the same alga often serves as host for several different fungi. Among the poisonous are Agaricus muscarius, Russula emetica, and Boletus lurdius. Boleti prefer woods as habitat.

Messrs. Cooke and Berkeley thus summarize the deleterious influence of fungi :—

On man, when eaten inadvertently ; poisonous also by the destruction of his legitimate food, and in producing and aggravating skin diseases.

On animals, by deteriorating or diminishing their food supplies, and by establishing themselves as parasites on some species.

On plants, by hastening the decay of timber, also establishing themselves as parasites, and impregnating the soil.

Fungi exert an important influence on the skin diseases of man. Favus or scald-head, called also porrigo, has its primary seat in the hair follicles ; Plica polonica occurs everywhere ; Tinea tonsurans, Alopecia, Sycosia, and Chionyphe are known, and hospital gangrene suspected.

Chionyphe Carteri, *Berkeley,* Mycetoma, *sp., H. Vandyke Carter,* is the fungus whose ravages cause the deeply-seated disease known as the Madura foot.

In domestic animals, as in cattle disease and in insects, as with species of Torrubia.

Dry-rot fungi are Merulius lacrymans, Polyporus hybridus.

Ergot is the sclerotioid condition of a species of the

Claviceps fungus which occurs on rye, on wheat, and on many of the wild grasses. It is employed medicinally.

In certain seasons ergot is much more common than in others, and farmers and graziers believe that in such seasons it is not uncommon for cattle to slip their young through feeding on ergotized grasses.

Mylitta, an underground fungus of the Neilgherry Hills, is closely allied to, if really distinct from, the so-called native bread of Tasmania. The natives of India call it the 'little man's bread,' in allusion to a tradition that the Neilgherries were once peopled by a race of pigmies. The small hard Mylitta, M. lapidescens, *Horn*, of China, is used there medicinally.

Peridermium Thomsoni, *Berkeley*, fungus attacks the Abies Smithiana on the Himalayas at elevation of 8000 feet. The leaves become reduced in length one-half, curved, and sprinkled, sometimes in double rows, with the large sort of this species, which at length prove fatal.

Polyporus anthelminticus, *Berkeley*, grows at the root of old bamboos, and is employed in Burma as an anthelmintic. P. fomentarius, *Fr.*, is the amadou or German tinder.

Puccinia graminis, the 'corn mildew,' is dimorphous, having a one-celled fruit (Trichobasis), as well as a two-celled fruit (Puccinia). The corn mildew and its accompanying 'rust' occur wherever corn is cultivated, whether in Australia or on the slopes of the Himalaya. The same may be said of 'smut,' for Ustilago is as common in Asia and America as in Europe. Dr. Cooke has seen it on numerous grasses, as well as on barley from the Panjab; also a species different from Ustilago maydis on the male florets of maize, from the same locality; and in 1870, one form of Ustilago made its appearance on rice, and is said to have affected a considerable portion of the standing rice crop in the vicinity of Diamond Harbour. It was described as constituting, in some of the infested grains, a whitish, gummy, interlaced, thread-like mycelium, growing at the expense of the tissues of the affected organs, and at la t becoming converted into a more or less coherent mass of spores, of a dirty green colour, on the exterior of the d formed grains. Beneath the outer coating the aggregated spores are of a bright orange-red; the central portion has a vesicular appearance, and is white in colour. 'Bunt' is another pest (Tilletia caries), which occupies the whole farinaceous portion of the grains of wheat.

Sorghum and the small millets are liable to attacks from allied parasites.

Sclerotium stipitatum, *Curr.*, occurs in nests of the white ant; the people suppose it to possess medicinal virtues.

Stilbum and Isaria, genera of fungi, occur in Ceylon.

Torrubia, a parasite genus of the fungi, of which twenty-five species are known; one seen in New Guinea on a species of coccus. Dr. Hooker found two in the Khasia Mountains. One American species occurs at Darjeling, and two in China. They kill their insect hosts. Torrubia sinensis, *Tul.*, of China, is developed on dead caterpillars; it is valued there medicinally. T. Taylori grows from the caterpillar of a large moth of Australia; and in New Zealand T. Robertsii attacks the larva of Hepialus virescens.

Botrytis Bassiana is a fungus which attacks and destroys the living insect.—*Dr. Cooke and the Rev. Mr. Berkeley; Dr. Cooke in the Economic Records of the India Office.*

G

Gæana maculata, one of the family Cicadidæ, is black with yellow spots.

Galeodes araneoides, one of the Solpugidæ, a family of the class Arachnida, is a great spider of the Central Asia steppes. They move abroad at night; seize and eat all weaker creatures, birds, bats, musk rats. G. fatalis has been known to kill a sparrow. There are thirty to thirty-five species, and they attack and eat their own species. Camels and sheep are said to die from their attacks.

Gamasus telarius (or Acarus telarius) is the scarlet mite or red spider. It pierces and imbibes the juices of the poppy leaves, and envelopes them in a delicate but closely-woven web, which so checks transpiration, that ultimately the plant becomes dry and withered. It avoides the poppy in its milk-sap stage. It is most abundant in hot, dry seasons.—*J. Scott.*

Ghoon is a Hindi generic name for the wood-boring Xylophagi. Nothing comes amiss to them,—bamboos, cereal grains, dried drugs, cheroots, pasteboard, books, timber, and even furniture made up of the light woods, although painted and in daily use, will be attacked and eaten by them; but it is the spongy and soft woods and the white or sap-wood that they attack. Natives of India destroy the ghoon by immersing the affected articles in water for some weeks.—*R. T.*

Girwi. A blight or rust of Hindustan causing the grain crops to assume a brick-dust colour. It awaits identification.

Glossina morsitans, *Westw.,* the tse-tse or spear-fly, is called Zebud in the Chaldean version of the Bible, Zimb in the Arabian version, and Tsaltsalya in the Ethiopian; the Greeks give it the name of Cynomya, and the negroes of Tse-tse. It is mentioned in Isa. vii. 18. This insect is one of the Muscidæ. It usually frequents the bushes and reeds on the borders of marshes. It is larger than a common fly, and of a whitish-yellow colour. The horse, the ox, and the dog, after they have been attacked by this insect, waste away and die in the course of a few days; those which are fat and in good condition soon die, while the others drag on a miserable existence for some weeks. Three or four flies are sufficient to produce these disastrous results. The blood of the animals which die is altered and diminished in quantity.—*M. T.*

Golunda Ellioti, the coffee rat.—See Coffee; Mammalia.

Gonda, of Hindustan, is very destructive to growing pulse. It needs to be determined.

Gossypium herbaceum. The cotton plant is attacked by species of Aphis, Arctia Horsfieldii, Cicadella (Typhlocyba), the larvæ of one of the Chrysomelidæ, Depressaria gossypiella, *Saunders,* Endioptis Indica, etc. From the larvæ of the Depressaria, the United States Agricultural Commissioner states that one-fourth of the cotton crop of India is sometimes lost. Now, allowing annually one pound weight of raw cotton to each of its 250,000,000, this at 3 annas the pound represents a value of in round numbers Rs. 4,50,00,000. Add to this the exported 4,189,718 cwt. in 1885–86, value Rs. 10,77,72,041, the cotton grown in India may be 6,421,950 cwt., value about sixteen crore. The cotton worm of the United States is the Aleta argillacea, *Buchner,* the Noctua xylona, *Say.* Their cotton bug or cotton stainer is the Dydercus suturellus, *Schif.*

The year 1877 in the United States was an unusual

harvest, nevertheless the loss in the cotton crop was estimated by their Board of Agriculture at 15,000,000 dollars.

In the North-Western Provinces caterpillars are often very destructive of growing cotton, sometimes stripping a field entirely of its leaves ; and an immense deal of loss results from the ravages of a smal white grub called 'sūndi,' which lives within the pod. Stagnant water, especially at the commencement of its growth, is most harmful. Rain, when the pods begin to open, is also very damaging, as the fibre becomes discoloured and rotten. Early frosts may altogether terminate the picking season a month or six weeks before it would otherwise have ended, and hence the desire to get the cotton seed into the ground as soon as possible.

Cotton plants in Southern India were described by Dr. Shortt as subject to the attacks of a kind of mildew, but it was found to be a diseased condition formerly classed with fungi, under the name of Erineum. A species of Torula attacks cotton pods after they are ripe.— *D. & F.*— *Vern. Kapas ; C. & B.*

Gracillaria coffeifolliella. Its larva mines the coffee leaves. It is very common.

Grain-weevil.—See Coleoptera; Curculionidæ; Calandra. —*Ch. O. W.*

Gryllidæ, an insect family of the order Orthoptera, having among its species the house, field, and mole crickets. The Acheta, Gryllotalpa vulgaris, Heliothis armigera, and Schizodactylus monstrosus are the more destructive. One species of Gryllus, of Northern India, called by the poppy cultivators 'phanga' or 'phunge,' is a voracious feeder when full grown, cropping the leaves and stalks of the poppy and other young plants, infesting the crops over large areas. They multiply and increase rapidly. A species of Lower Bengal, the 'gudhia,' attacks the young poppy plant in November and December.

Some species of Gryllus attack the young poppy plant in all its stages ; others follow the seed into granaries, and the Gryllotalpa vulgaris, with species of Acheta, Heliothis armigera, and Tetranychus papaveræ, take part in the work of destruction. Acheta campestris, A. domestica, and another species or variety in Bengal appear from the close of November to the middle of January. They rarely attack the poppy plant in its germinating stage, confining their attacks to the later stages of development of its root-leaf system. They are the 'jhengur' of Hindustan. A species of Acheta frequently commits sad havoc on the young poppy crops, extending in dry seasons from November to January, emerging during the night from their hiding-place in the soil. The insectivorous birds are great helps in their suppression, and dusting the plants with powdered charcoal and lime, or ashes and lime, is useful.—*J. Scott.*—See Cylindrodes ; Heliothis.

Gryllotalpa vulgaris is often a serious pest to the poppy, cutting over with its powerful mandibles considerably advanced plants. It makes very extensive and variously directed underground channels. The easiest mode of destroying them is to flood their haunt, and catch the insects as they emerge. It is a destructive creature of nocturnal habits. It seems to be known in Bengal as the goorgooria, or oo-chingra.—*J. Scott.*

H

Hæmopsis. Horse leech is a name applied to Hæmopsis sanguisuga, and to a species of Aulostomum. The latter is voracious; they feed on all creatures. Hæmopsis sanguisuga, *Moq.*, is met with in Sweden, in the south of Spain, in Portugal, and in Turkey. It is very common in the north of Africa, and is one of the main causes of disease in the animals of Algeria. It has feeble jaws, and can only penetrate mucous membranes. Hence the necessity for it to introduce itself into the natural cavities of oxen, horses, and other herbivora, camels, mules; and into the mouth, pharynx, nasal fossæ, and trachea of man when drinking water. There are three principal varieties of leeches employed medicinally in France. These are— 1st, the grey leech; 2nd, the green leech; 3rd, the dragon leech. The leeches in the damp climate of Assam cause much injury to travellers. They are small, and adhere to the legs in numbers, causing loss of blood and ulcers.

Land leeches of Ceylon are about an inch in length, and as fine as a knitting needle, but capable of distention to the size of a quill. A closely-woven cloth is needed to prevent their attack. The wound which they inflict is on the more tender and less exposed parts of the body, and on the fetlocks of horses; and the hill leech of the Sikkim streams is no less inimical.

Haltica has a species in Bengal very similar to the turnip-fly or turnip flea-beetle of Europe, H. nemorum. It feeds on the young leaves and flower-buds of the mustard.

Heliocopis cupido larvæ attack the cotton plant in its bud. The larvæ are dispersed by sprinkling ashes over the plant.

Heliothis armigera, one of the Gryllidæ, is very generally diffused through Upper Bengal, the North-Western Provinces, and the Panjab. It attacks the leaves and capsules of the poppy and all the various pulses, especially the mussoors (Ervum lens), chana (Cicer arietinum), and mutur (Pisum sativum), less frequently urhur (Cajanus Indicus), boring into poppy capsules, and feeding on the seeds. With the poppy, the caterpillars feed from the lower leaves up to the capsule, which they penetrate, and there pass into the pupa and perfect form, the male moth being of a pale orange colour, one female colouring being of a darker and another of a paler hue. But the imprisoned moth rarely makes its escape from the capsule; indeed, scarcely one in ten gets out; and they have vigilant foes in the mynas, which, perching on the bored capsules, watch the operations of the caterpillar, and should it appear at the aperture, the myna immediately strikes, and rarely fails in withdrawing it in whole or in part. Mr. John Scott asserts that neither this caterpillar nor any other with which he made experiments will attack the parts of the opium poppy when in any way replete with a normally concentrated milk - sap. Heliothis armigera suddenly in the season of 1877−78 attacked the poppy crops in the Patna and Shahabad districts. Careful hand - picking of the affected capsules was the only remedy suggested. It has, at different times, proved most destructive to cotton crops, eating into the capsules. The opium poppy is not supposed to be its natural food. One species occurs in Kashmir. —*J. Scott.*

Helminths living in man are of three orders :

1. NEMATODA.	2. TREMATODA.	3. CESTODA.
Ancylostomum duodenale. Ascaris lumbricoides. Ascar. alata. Filaria lentis, lymphatica, Medinensis, oculi. Spiroptera hominis. Strongylus longivaginatus. Strong. renalis. Trichina spiralis. Tricocephalus dispar.	Distoma Buskii. D. hepaticum. D. heterophya. D. lanceolatum. D. ophthalmobium. Festucaria lentis. Thecosoma sanguicola.	Bothriocephalus latus. Tænia communis; larva, Cysticercus cellulosa. T. nana. T. flavopunctata. T. echinococcus ; larva, Echinococcus veterinorum. T. inermis. T. acanthotrias ; larva, Cyst. acanthotrocus. T. dentalis ; larva, Echin. hominis. T. tenuicollis ; larva, Cyst. tenuicollis.

Those living in the alimentary canal are the Ancylostomum, Ascaris, Bothriocephalus, Oxyurus, Tænia, and Tricocephalus. Out of the alimentary canal are found the Distoma, Festucaria, Filaria, Spiroptera, Strongylus, and Thecosoma. Cysticerci are helmintha larvæ which are furnished with a caudal vesicle. There are three principal species. Cysticercus bovis is the measle of the ox ; it is the larva of the cestoid worm Tænia mediocanallata, a common form of tape-worm. It is in small segments, and each ripe segment of the tape-worm contains about 40,000 eggs. Tænia solium is the tape-worm derived from the pig ; it is an entozoon often causing severe ill-health. There is another which Dr. Cobbold supposes belongs to the sheep. They attain their position in man by his eating uncooked or ill-cooked food. Flesh food properly cooked may be eaten with safety. The prevalence of entozoa in military ration beef will be seen from the following extract record from Peshawar :—' Read Military

Department letter, 8th October 1869, forwarding statement of cattle found infected during the month of August 1869: out of 840 slaughtered, 31 were found to have cysts, 19 of these having presented at Peshawar. Statement for September 1869: out of 732 slaughtered, 15 were infected, 7 detected at Peshawar. Statement for October 1869 : out of 390 slaughtered, 6 infected.'

Helopeltis Antonii, *Wood-Mason.* Tea-bug or mosquito blight. Other species are H. braconiformis and nigra, Waigiou; collaris, pellucida, from Philippines; podagrica and theivora of Assam.—See Tea-bug.

Hemileia vastatrix, an entophyte, causing the leaf disease of the coffee planters of the south of India and Ceylon. It is the fungus of the coffee-leaf disease. Its spore (Uredo spore), germinating on the damp under-surface of the coffee leaf, emits a short delicate tube which sends a prolongation through a stoma, and the further development of this results in the production of the intercellular mycelium. The mycelium of Hemileia not only robs the leaf of valuable materials, but it diverts the flow of nutritive substances, and by occupying space in the tissues of the plants, it prevents these tissues from fulfilling functions of service to the coffee tree. It has been one of the greatest scourges with which the coffee enterprise of Southern India has had to contend. The yield of fruit diminished. Prior to 1874, the average yield for five years in Ceylon had been 4·5 cwt. per acre, but in the five succeeding years the yield was only 2·9 cwt.

Hemiptera, or bugs, an order of insects; among its destroying genera are the Aphis and Coccus of the two families Aphidæ or plant-lice and gall insects.—See Bug.

Hippobosca equina, *Linn.,* the horse-fly, is an insect belonging to the order Diptera, and to the family Pupipara. This insect settles on horses and cattle, generally beneath the tail near the anus; they select the parts which are devoid of hair. It is known in the New Forest of England as the forest fly. With its sucker it punctures the skin of horses and cattle, and eagerly sucks their blood. Man is not free from their attacks.— See Fly.

Hoplosternus. A species of this genus is the common chafer of Queensland. Its grub destroys the roots of the sugar-cane, causing the leaves to become brown and dry up; the growth of the cane is arrested, and the first high wind knocks it over. In this manner whole fields of cane are killed. In the early stage, the larvæ are engaged in gnawing the root. In November and December, the chafers, fully developed, appear above ground in swarms; inactive during the day, but feeding eagerly at night.—*L. R.*

Hordeum vulgare, *Linn.* The most striking of the diseases to which Indian barley is liable is that commonly known as ' kandwa,' which is the result of the attack of a fungus closely allied to that which causes ' smut ' in English corn - fields. The first symptoms of the disease is distortion of the ear and swelling out of the stalk joints. Then a blackish dust makes its appearance on the ear and at the stalk joints, which rapidly spreads over them and entirely destroys the grain. There are very few barley fields in which some of these distorted, charred-looking heads cannot be detected, and they are especially numerous in seasons of good winter rain.—*D. & F.*—*Vern. Jao.*

Huechys sanguinea, one of the Cicadidæ, a small black species, with blood-red abdomen, said to be a powerful vesicant.

Hylesinus fraxini, *Fabr.*, is the ash bark beetle of England. In India the Hylesini attack the bamboo and the pine. Mr. Thompson has known, in Dehra Doon, a species of Hylesinus attack and so entirely eat the poles and rafters of houses made of the sal tree, as to cause the roofs of the buildings to fall in ; and a similar occurrence in a building in the hills, in which the ' Cheer ' pine, Pinus longifolia, was used.—*R. T.*

Hymenoptera, an order in which naturalists arrange several insects, some of them useful, others injurious to man and his industries, as species of the genus Tenthredo, family Scurifera; also the Cynips family; and the Xylocopa wood borers of the family Mellifera or bees. Hymenoptera comprise the gall insect, ichneumon flies, sand wasps, mason wasps, mining wasps, stinging ants, common ants, wasps, hornets, carpenter bees, honey bees, and dammer bees,—almost all of them injurious. They mostly have stings with which to protect themselves, and the pain from the thrust of that of the wasp, the bee, the hornet, or the ichneumon is considerable, death even resulting from the attacks of a multitude of bees. Even large birds like the myna carefully fly off to avoid the hornet's attacks.

I

Icerya sacchari is the waxy sugar-cane louse, known also as Le Pou à Poché Blanche, of Queensland and Mauritius. Mr. H. Ling Roth supposes that it is milked by a small black ant, Formica rufonigra, in the same manner as species of the Aphides are by other ants. He considers it to be the cause of injury to sugar-cane.

Indigofera tinctoria, *Linn.* The most dreaded source

of damage to the indigo plant is continued wet weather, which renders the plants tall and woody, without much foliage, and by a kind of etiolation prevents the proper development of the dye property. A proper allowance of sunlight is as necessary to the production of the dye as water is to the growth of the plant.—*D. & F.*— *Vern. Nil.*

Itch.—See Sarcoptes.

Ixodes, the ticks, a genus of Acarina, are parasitic on most animals. I. ricinus is common on the dog, I. bovis on cattle and deer; I. brevipes occurs in Ceylon. Europe, Africa, and America have other species, all of them hurtful. The sheep tick, however, the Melophagus ovinus, is an apterous fly of the family Hippoboscidæ.

J

Jackal.—See Mammal.

K

Kadhya, or **Gudhia** in the language of Hindustan, is an insect more or less troublesome to various products of the fields and gardens of Northern India. It has a rough, warty, or shagreened skin, of a dirty ash-grey colour. It needs identification.

L

Lachnosterna. A genus of Lamellicorn Coleoptera of the family Melolonthidæ. The species are very numerous in India, and do much mischief to trees. Lachnosterna pinguis of Walker, ' the yellow-bellied cockchafer,' a brown species, about an inch long, injures the coffee trees in Dimbula, Ceylon, and in parts of India.—See Coffee Trees.

Lady-birds.—See Coleoptera ; Coccinellidæ.

Lamellicornes, an insect family of the order Coleoptera. Its genera most hurtful to living and dead vegetable substances are the Euchirus and Lucanus.

Lathyrus sativus, *Linn.*, is the lathyros of the Greeks, and cicercula of the Romans. It is a coarse kind of pea, notorious for its effect in producing paralysis if eaten in quantity. This has been ascribed to its nitrogenous constituents, in which it is excessively abundant. Colonel Sleeman, in 1833–34, found half the youth of both sexes of villages in East Oudh affected with it, and many had entirely lost the use of their lower limbs. The widespread occurrence of paralysis in Sind, after a season in which this crop was grown in an exceptionally large area, attracted considerable attention ; and in the Azamgarh district of Hindustan, where it forms an important item of diet, similar effects have been observed. Horses and bullocks when much fed on it are equally liable to lose the use of their limbs. Cases of paralysis among the horses in the military station of Almora were traced to the fraudulent admixture of this pea with the gram supplied for the use of the troops.—*D. & F.*—*Vern. Kasāri.*

Latrodectes lugubris, the kara kurt or black worm of the Kirghiz, is about the size of a finger nail. It can jump several feet, and its bite is very venomous.—*Schuyler,* ii. p. 123.

Lecanium, a genus of the Coccidæ family of insects.

In Europe, L. hesperidum attacks the orange. Lecanium nigrum, one of the two black insects of the Ceylon coffee planters. L. coffeæ is the brown or scaly bug.—See Coffee Trees.

Leeches.—See Hæmopsis.

Lepisma, *sp.*, the fish insect which infests books. This and Chelifer tailless scorpion eat the soft-bodied acari that injure books.—See Book-worm.

Leptocorisa Bengalensis, *Westwood,* L. acuta, *Thunberg,* L. varicornis, *Fabricus;* Munju vandu of the Tamil people of Tinnevelly; Gandi of Assam. About January 1886, Mr. Lee-Warner, Collector of the Tinnevelly district of the Madras Presidency, brought to the notice of the Director of Revenue Settlement, that 50 per cent. of the rice crops nearly throughout the Srivilliputur taluk had been injured by the Leptocorisa Bengalensis. This insect belongs to the family Coreidæ of the order Rhynchota, the vast majority of the members of which live upon the juices of plants, a few only, such as the common bed-bug, attacking animals. This bug was described in 1837 by Professor Westwood, in his *Catalogue of Hemiptera in the Collection of the Rev. F. W. Hope.* If the synonyms prove all to refer to one and the same species, it will be found to range, under slight variations of form, from India and Ceylon, through Burma and the Malay countries, to Australia, wherein it affects low-lying lands suited to rice cultivation, only occasionally creeping a short distance up contiguous hill-sides.— *W.-M.*

Leptura. A small species of this insect genus has been observed in numbers in the logs of the harder woods of Kamaon and Garhwal. A larger species has also been seen. The genus belongs to the family Longicornes, order Coleoptera.— *R. Thompson.*

Lice are classed by naturalists among the Anoplura, and include the feather and hair-eating family Mallophaga, with its genera Menopon, Trinoton, Docophorus, Nirmus, Goniocotes, Gonioides, Lipeurus, Ornithobius, Trichodectes, Hæmatomyzus, Hæmatopynus, Phthirius, and the true lice genus Pediculus, which has P. capitis and its varieties. Lice of different species, some of different genera, attack birds, sheep, the dog, cat, ox, elephant, and the monkey. Turkeys are the hosts of two species of lice, one named Lipeurus meleagridis or polytrapezius, lives principally on the wings ; the other, Gonioides stylifer, prefers the head, neck, and breast of the bird.—*Morton's Cyclopædia.*

Ligurus ruficeps is the sugar-cane beetle of the United States. It is a stout black beetle, half an inch long, which bores into the stalk of the sugar-cane underground. It has not been traced in India.

Lixus. A longish weevil, seemingly a species of Lixus, one of the divisions into which the Longirostres have been made, was constantly found by Mr. Thompson under the bark of felled logs. It bores with facility through the softer parts of wood.

Longicornes or Capricorn beetles, a family of the order Coleoptera. Its more injurious genera are the Cerambyx, Lamia, Leptura, Monochamus, Prionus, and Saperda.

Loranthus. The epiphytic Loranthaceæ parasites injured the Acacia melanoxylon of the Neilgherries. The parasite covered the larger branches, diverting the sap.—See Parasites.

Lucanidæ, or stag-beetles, are pre-eminently wood-feeders. They live, in their larva stage, in the interior of the trunks of large trees. Species of the genus occur throughout India. Mr. Hope, writing on the insects collected by Dr. W. Griffith in Assam, mentions Lucanus

Forsteri, L. Rafflesii, L. Spencii, L. curvidens, L. bulbosus, and L. punctiger. The Lucanus cervus, when in felled logs, are easily killed by immersion in cold water, or by pouring scalding water into their hole. No grub can withstand this operation.

The stag-beetles in India are numerous, and common as to individuals, and are, of the whole order of wood-beetles, the most destructive to living trees. Their larvæ live for three or four years in the interior of trunks of oak, and about Naini Tal barely one in ten of the trees escape their ravages. These and the larvæ of Prionus beetles seem exclusively to attach themselves there to the oak as their habitation. They bore to the heart of the stem, in winding passages. Male stag-beetles have been found feeding on the renewed bark (after shaving) of Cinchona succirubra trees, in Maskeliya, Ceylon. The female has much shorter mandibles, and is said to use them in forming a hole in the trunks of trees for the reception of its eggs. Mr. Westwood says (i. p. 187) the perfect insect feeds on the honey-dew upon the leaves of the oak; they also feed upon the sap exuding from the wounds of trees, which they lap up with their finely-ciliated maxillæ and lower lip. It has been supposed that the larva of this insect, which chiefly hides in the willow and oak, remaining in that state several years, is the animal so much esteemed by the Romans as a delicacy, and named cossus. The injury which it causes is often very considerable, boring not only into the solid wood, but also into the roots of the tree. A stag-beetle received from Maskeliya was a male with immense mandibles, and greatly resembled Lucanus cervus, the common stag-beetle of Europe.—*R. T.*

Lycosa tarantula. Tarantula spiders are poisonous.

They belong to the genus Lycosa of Latreille. They are characterized by having the eyes arranged in an elongated quadrilateral form. There are several species.—See Araneidæ.——*M. T.*

M

Maggot. Mr. (Sir) H. B. Loch mentions (p. 183) that in all the Chinese prisons a small maggot lodges a few inches under the surface, and is a scourge of the prisoners. Maggot, grub, and caterpillar are popular terms applied to the larvæ of certain insects.

Makora, in the vernacular of Hindustan, a generic term for four kinds of larvæ of longicorn beetles, depredators on the Shorea robusta and the pine.

Mamestra papaverorum attacks the growing poppy in February and March. They become entrapped in the maturing capsules.—*R. T.*

Mammals.—The bear, boar, elephant, galeopithecus, hyæna, jackal, porcupine, pteropus or flying fox, cynopterus, shrew, and wolf, all inflict injury on man and his products. In 1882–83, in British India, the numbers of persons killed by wild beasts and snakes were 22,905, and of cattle so killed 47,478, as under :—

	Persons.	Cattle.
By Elephants, . . .	63	36
,, Tigers, . . .	985	16,563
,, Leopards, . . .	217	19,064
,, Bears, ...	119	315
,, Wolves, . . .	287	6,704
,, Hyænas, . . .	28	1,181
,, Others, . . .	1,139	1,971
,, Snakes, . . .	20,067	1,644

	Wild Beasts Destroyed, 1882-83.	Rewards Paid. Rs.
Elephants, . . .	4	100
Tigers, ...	1,825	48,487
Leopards, ...	4,349	64,653
Bears, ...	1,599	7,039
Wolves, ...	6,239	21,555
Hyænas, ...	1,569	5,223
Other wild beasts, . . .	4,304	4,948
Total, . . .	19,889	1,52,005
Snakes, ...	412,782	22,353

In India, after droughts and famines, the locusts and the Golunda meltada field rats migrate in myriads, eating up every green thing. Such migration of rats occurred in the Peninsula in 1826. After the famine of 1877–1878, the Bombay Government gave a rupee for every hundred tails, and it is said 11,000,000 were destroyed. In 1875–76 rats infested the watersheds of the Salwin and Sitang. According to Bancroft, rats were driven from parts of Jamaica, utterly exterminated by an ant, to which the colonists gave the name of Tom Raffles, but the remedy was worse than the disease. But what India has most to dread is drought.

In the Indian famine of 1877–78, in the Peninsula of India, millions of the inhabitants, and the bulk of their horned cattle, perished. Mr. Forbes tells us, on the authority of the *Batavia Handelsblad*, that in Java the years 1877 and 1878 were marked by great droughts. From that of the latter year the loss on the coffee estates from the Hemileia vastatrix, or leaf blight, was ten million guilders ; on sugar, seven ; on tobacco, five ; and on rice, fifteen—equal in all to a loss, in English money, of £3,000,000. Along with these disastrous seasons came a terrible epizootic among the buffaloes, which had not disappeared in the middle of 1883. Not only was the coffee blighted, but the grass meadows and the forest trees were covered with a fungoid disease. In Sumatra, not alone the buffaloes suffered; numbers of the elephants, the deer, and the wild pigs died in the forests, and by preying on the dying herds even tigers fell victims to the pestilence. In Timor, also, in the higher parts of the island, the cattle were attacked; while in the southern plains, the pigs and the horses, which there run wild in herds, were found scattered about in the forest dead.

The elephants, sometimes solitary, sometimes in herds, at times do much injury to villages.

The shrews passing over food articles so taint them with the musky odour as to make them useless.

The porcupine does much harm to plantations.

The wolves, wild dogs, and jackals hunt in packs, but there is no record of the wild dog destroying man. Not so of the other two.

In 1874, Dy. Surgeon General John Shortt proposed a very effective mode of destroying tigers, to which effect might be given.

In India the wild boar frequently occupies a patch of sugar-cane.

While man and domesticated animals have to be protected against the attacks of carnivorous mammals, the horned cattle of India demand from man a special care. They are the agriculturists' chief wealth; and anthrax, rinderpest, dysentery, and epizootic aphtha inflict vast losses. Beginnings have been made. The Madras Government has (1886) an Inspector and Deputy-Inspector of Cattle Diseases, with fourteen local inspectors; and the Glanders and Farcy Act (Act xx. of 1879) of the Government of India was framed to stamp out these diseases.

In India the most important diseases of horned stock are rinderpest, foot-and-mouth disease, hoven, quarter-ill, pleuro - pneumonia, *bhooknee* or purging, cystic disease, throat swelling, and anthrax.

Rinderpest is the designation given, in the *Indian Cattle Plagues Report*, to the highly-infectious disease which Dr. Gilchrist, in 1848, described under the term ' Burra Azār,' or great sickness. The Burra Azār occurs in an epizootic form over all India, Burma, and Ceylon, but has various native names. It is highly infectious, and recovery is rare. ' The yearly loss is very serious, and to be counted by hundreds of thousands.' The natives ' confess their powerlessness to treat this disease ;' and the India Commissioners can only recommend a quarantine isolation of the sick cattle, burying those that die, and disinfecting of localities. Rinderpest, cholera, and small-pox ' are hot-weather diseases ; they do occur simultaneously, but not invariably, necessarily, or even very frequently.' ' Inoculation from this distemper resulted in the development of a varioloid disease.'

Foot-and-mouth disease does not cause great mortality. The deaths are caused by inability to eat owing to disease of the mouth, or to severe ulceration of the feet owing to the development of maggots. The mouth is recommended to be washed with a solution of alum (10 grs. to 1 oz.), and the feet to be treated with camphor and oil or carbonic acid and oil. It is the Aphtha epizootica.

Hoven is an exceedingly common form of fatal disease among Indian cattle. It consists of suffocation from over-distention of the rumen, or with food or flatus. Tapping is not known to the people, and they mostly think the disease incurable. A large aggregate amount of stock yearly falls victims to this preventible and curable disease.

F

Quarter-ill or quarter-evil, the black-leg of Scotland, occurs in Jessore. It has its origin in causes which may affect the members of a herd in common, and thus may assume the aspect of an epizootic. It is often fatal.

Pleuro-pneumonia is known in the Panjab and Sind; and, although not so general or destructive as rinderpest or *bhooknee*, the disease is a common and destructive one. It appears to be more sporadic than epizootic. The people do not think it is contagious; but this is not in accordance with the opinion in Great Britain, South Africa, and Australia, and it is recommended to act upon the contagious view.

Bhooknee or purging is an endemic disease of the Panjab, caused by improper diet and watering, and occurring to an exceptionally severe extent in an exceptionally dry year.

Cyst disease, Echinococcus veterinorum, is the larva of Tænia echinococcus, and is prevalent among all Indian cattle. Tænia medio-canellata is the beef helminth.

Throat disease is epizootic and fatal among Indian cattle. It was not seen by the Commissioners, but was surmised to be a swelling of the parotid and submaxillary glands, or an effusion of blood into the subcutaneous cellular tissue of the neck and dewlap. The people fire the parts.

The males of the larger of the mammalia have fierce combats for supremacy, and the defeated combatant, driven from the herd, leads a solitary life, always morose, and frequently mischievous. In Ceylon the elephants so apart are known as the 'rogue,' but the term is applied to the similarly separated males of the wild buffalo, the hippopotamus, and sperm whale, and in that state they often go out of their way to attack man.

The Ursus Malayanus, Sciurus palmarum or palm squirrel, the common rat, and the palm martin, Paradoxurus typus, are all accused of destroying the cocoanut.

Deer will not enter fields when the safflower has been sown intermixed with the cereals or millets.

Dogs refuse to sleep on rugs beneath which mint has been laid.—*Commissioners' Report*, 1871.—See Helminths.

Mango Worm. *The Indian Agriculturist* of the 19th December 1885 quotes the *Reis and Rayyot* native newspaper as stating that ' the fly is so tenacious of life that it thrives within the heart of the fruit. You cut a fruit apparently sound, without a spot on the surface, when, lo! the fly issues out of the interior and buzzes about you. These insects have degraded the East Bengal mango for at least more than half a century, and yet no notice has been taken of the matter.' The scientific name of this insect is a desideratum.

Measle.—See Helminths.

Melolonthidæ. In the tea plantations of the Dehra Doon, a small beetle occurred, supposed to be one of this family. It lay two or three inches in the ground during the day. It was dug up in bushels and destroyed.

Melolontha vulgaris is the common cockchafer of Europe. M. Reiset estimated that, in 1865–66, agricultural produce to the value of more than a million sterling was destroyed in the Department of Seine Inférieure. There are many species belonging to the Melolonthideous or Cetonideous genera in Ceylon. Under the name of white grub were included the larvæ of various Melolonthidæ, the cockchafers of Ceylon, which do much harm to coffee plantations, young and old, by eating the roots of the trees. Mr. J. L. Gordon, of Rambodde, considered the white grub

to be by far the greatest enemy of the coffee trees with
which the planter had to contend, as he.never knew a
single tree recover after their attack; and he adds that
they had destroyed, at Rambodde, in two years, between
eight and ten thousand trees of fine old coffee.   Mr.
Gordon used to dig up the soil at the foot of the trees
and take out such grubs as he could find.—*R. Thompson.*

Melophagus ovinus is the sheep tick.—See Ixodes.

Mites.   Cheese mites can be eaten with impunity.—See
Acarina.

Mollusca inflict injury on man and his industries.
Woodward, writing in England, says : ' All the land snails
are vegetable feeders, and their depredations are but too
well known to the gardener and farmer ; many a crop of
winter corn and spring tares has been wasted by the
ravages of the small grey slug.'   ' They hold white mustard
in abhorrence, and fast or shift their quarters while that
crop is on the ground.'   Dilute lime-water and very
weak alkaline solutions are more fatal to snails than
even salt.

The genus Octopus, one of the Cephalopoda, destroys
many of the crustacea, and its long arms cling to the
arms and legs of people in the water.   The habits of the
predatory mollusca of India await examination.   Among
the mollusca, the cone species, the genus pleurotoma,
inflict bites which inflame and become dangerous.

Monochamus soongna, a Longicorn beetle, attacks the
' seemul' Bombax heptaphyllum, the ' soongna ' Moringa
pterygosperma, and the 'roongrah' Erythrina suberosa.
It is a magnificent beetle of the tribe Cerambycidæ ; and
its large larvæ, armed with powerful mandibles, are very
destructive to the woods of these trees.   Out of a six-
foot log of moringa, Mr. Thompson collected forty-three

perfect beetles, five or six pupæ, and about a dozen larvæ. Another monochamous beetle attacks the Butea frondosa and the wild willow, Salix tetrasperma, entering the trunk and boring in all directions. A third species has its pupæ inclosed in solid cocoons made of a substance resembling lime, with a shell fully one-sixteenth of an inch in thickness, quite hard and firm. Its larvæ and pupæ are both found in the woods of the Odina wodier and Bombax heptaphyllum.—*R. Thompson.*

Mosquito blight. Have toon trees anything to do with mosquito blight ? The manager of the Chenga Tea Estate noted that, ' both in the hills and here, these trees are always more or less blighted the whole year round, and that the tea bushes under them and near by are always the first to be attacked.' Wherever toon trees are on the garden, he adds, the blight is worst, ' so that I would recommend every tree being cut down, as they are perfectly useless and valueless—all leaves and small branches to be burned.'——See Helopeltis ; Tea-bug.

Moths known to science number 40,000 to 50,000.—See Coffee Trees.

Muscidæ. A family of dipterous insects, including the common house-fly, the blue-bottle, the flesh-fly, the green-bottle fly, the tse-tse, the phorides, œstrides. The number of dipterous insects on the globe is estimated at 150,000 to 160,000.—See Flies.

Mycoidea parasitica, *D. D. Cunningham.* A cryptogam plant observed at Calcutta on the leaves of the Camellia Japonica as a destructive sloughing blight; occurring also on tea and rhododendron leaves, ferns, and crotons.

Mygalidæ.—See Araneidæ.

Myrmeleon, or ant lion, are species of the Myr-meleontidæ, and the genera Myrmeleon and Palpares.

They are useful to man. They excavate cup-shaped hollows, at the bottom of which they lie in ambush and seize the insects that fall down the smooth sides.

N

Necrophorus.—See Coleoptera; Silphidæ.

Necera lepida, *Cramer,* the Limacodes graciosa, *West.,* short, broad, pale-green, with black spines, which feeds on the Carissa jasminiflora, stings with fury. It occupies also the Thespesia populnea, and at a certain stage of its growth descends by a silken thread and hurries away.

Nepa cinerea, *Linn.,* commonly called water scorpion or water spider, is a hemipterous insect, belonging to the section Heteroptera, and to the family Hydrocores.

Neuroptera, the lace-wing order of insects, to which belong the termes, white ants, of the family Planipennes. The larvæ attack growing and dead vegetable matter. Examples of this class are May flies, dragon flies, winged white ants.

Nicotiana tabacum, *Linn.,* and N. rustica, *Linn.,* are said in the North-Western Provinces never to be attacked by insects. The leaves occasionally suffer from a grey mildew called 'kapti' in the Azamgarh district.—*D. & F.—Vern. Tamaka.*

Noctua exclamationis, the khumwa of the Assamese, the heart and dart moth, is the common pest of field and garden crops. In the caterpillar stage it attacks the young poppy plant, cutting across the stalk close to the surface of the soil, and in a night will cut down fifty to a hundred or more plants. The caterpillar is nearly cylindrical, and 1½ to 2 inches long.

Noctua segetum is the corn dart moth of England. In India it or a variety or allied species is known as the khumwa; in its larva state infests the young poppy. It gnaws out the stalk close to the ground, and a single caterpillar, in the course of a night's raid, will cut down from fifty to a hundred or more plants. It is the most destructive of the insect foes of the young poppy, but not unfrequently extends its ravages to the adjoining crops of mustards, pulses, etc. It is checked by dusting with a mixture of quicklime and ashes.

A species of noctua in its caterpillar state in Bengal attacks the young sprouts of the potato-plant, boring into them under the surface of the soil, and consuming the soft interior parts, so that the whole shoot withers and dies.

Noctua, *sp.*, observed by Mr. J. Scott at Medapore in gardens, had a caterpillar 1 to 1½ inch long, with a small brown horny head, six pectoral, eight abdominal, and two anal feet. They pass into the pupa state in a thin webby cocoon, formed on the lower surface of the poppy leaves. The moth emerges in from 14 to 20 days, measuring about 2½ inches from tip to tip of the forewings. Its caterpillar feeds on the leaves of the cabbage and the green leaves of the poppy.—*J. Scott.*

O

Œcidium Thomsoni infests the Abies Smithiana fir-tree.

Œdipoda cinerascens and Œ. migratoria are species of locusts, the latter is the oriental locust. They are exceedingly voracious, and when they appear in great numbers, they do much damage in cultivated ground.

While still in their larval state they travel in search of nourishment ; but their great wanderings are in flight when they have attained their perfect state.   They clear everything off the surface of the ground as completely as if it had been visited by fire, and have sometimes caused disastrous famines.   Southey in *Thalaba* says :—

> ' Onward they come, a dark continuous cloud
> Of congregated myriads, numberless,
> The rushing of whose wings was as the sound
> Of a broad river headlong in its course,
> Plunged from a mountain summit, or the roar
> Of a wild ocean in the autumn storm,
> Shattering its billows on a shore of rocks.'

They have repeatedly invaded Northern India, Sind, Rajputana, the Bombay Dekhan, and the Ceded Districts ; and Major Moore mentions that on one occasion they devastated Maharashtra over a width of 500 miles. The starling, Pastor roseus, is their great destroyer ; but in their larva state, as they travel onwards, trenches are dug in their front, into which they fall and are covered over.   Swarms appear in the Ceded Districts in May and June, depositing their eggs, about 70 in each hole, and three months is the period of incubation.

Œstrides.   Œstrus bovis, *L.*, the ox œstrus ; Œ. ovis, *L.*, the sheep œstrus or Cephalemyea ovis ; Œ. equi, *L.*, the horse œstrus.   Œ. elephantis takes up its abode in the stomach of the elephant.   Œ. equi and Œ. ovis cause the death of many of their victims.

Œstrus equi occurs in the south of Europe and Persia. It is a dipterous insect.   Its eggs are deposited on the hair of the horse, and licked into the stomach, and when complete the insects pass through the canal.   Œ. ovis, of Europe and the East Indies, lays its eggs in the nostrils of the sheep, and the worm from it occupies the frontal sinuses, and gives rise to fatal diseases.

Opium. A yellow mould resembling Sporotrichum has been seen (*C. & B.*) in the heart of a ball of opium, and a white mould also occurs on opium, and more than one species is troublesome in the opium factories of India. —*C. & B.*—See Poppy.

P

Palm trees are attacked by the Rhynchophorus palm-arum, the Euchirus longimanus, chafer, the Sphæno-phorus planipennis, weevil of Ceylon; and in Malacca, the cocoa-nut trees are further injured by the Xylotrupes gideon and Oryctes rhinoceros.

Panicum frumentaceum, *Roxb.*, is liable to damage from excessive rain, and suffers from blight. It is sown a little before or after the rains break. The crop is a bountiful one.—*Vern. Sawan.*

Panicum miliaceum, *Linn.*, is sown in March, and ripens towards the middle of May. It is very liable to damage from the hot winds.—*D. & F.*—*Vern. Cheehna.*

Paraponyx oryzalis, *Wood-Mason.* The Burmese people say that their paddy is liable to four blights, which they name Y-wet-pyat-po, Pin-bo or Oo-shouk-po, Sat-mee, and Palan-byoo, and these have been described by Mr. Mouna Too. The Palan-byoo blight of Burma is caused by the Paraponyx oryzalis of Mr. Wood-Mason, who says it is a small insect belonging to the hetero-cerous division of the order Lepidoptera. In two stages of its metamorphosis, it is known to the Burmese as the Tein-doung-bo and the Palan-byoo, the one being the caterpillar and the other the pupa or chrysalis. The caterpillar is about 7 millim., or rather more than $\frac{1}{4}''$ long. The pupa is fusiform, 9·5 millim. long by 2·25 millim. broad. The cocoon is 12 millim. long and 2·5 broad. It is composed of whitish silk. The Paraponyx oryzalis is an animal of considerable interest to naturalists, inasmuch as in its larval stages it is specially modified for a purely aquatic life ; in the caterpillar stage, breathing water by means of tracheal gills.— *W.-M.*

Parasites are animals or vegetables. The former, for the greater part of their life, live in or on the bodies of other animals. Vegetable parasites attach themselves to other plants, whose juices they absorb. Among the parasitic vegetables are several fungi. The genera of the order Loranthaceæ are all parasitic ; the mistletoe, Viscum album, is found on the alder, elm, maple, olive, mulberry, poplar, walnut, and willow in the Himalaya and the Suliman range ; V. monoicum is parasitic on Elæodendron and other trees. Arceuthobium oxycedri grows on the branches of the Juniperus excelsa, often killing the branch. Species of Loranthus on the Neilgherries destroyed plantations of Australian acacia, attacking the peach and other trees ; while, in the Sub-Himalayan tracts, the oak, platanus, salix, rhododendron, mango, peach, and pear all suffer from other Loranthi.

Animal parasites attack man and other animals. Among them may be named Acari, *sp.*, the Argas, Ascarides, Ancylostomum, Bothriocephalus, Cysticerci, Echinococci, Filaria, Fistularia, flea, flukes, harvest-bug, Helmintha, louse, Œstridea, Oxyurus, Sarcoptus, Spiroptera, Strongylus, Tænia, Thecosoma, tick, Tricocephalus. The bites of all are painful, many of them dangerous. In classifying parasites, they are usually arranged as Endo-parasites or Entozoa when they infest the internal organs, such as the stomach and bowels, lungs, liver, kidneys, etc. ; and as Ecto-parasites or Epizoa when found on the external surface of the body.

There are at least other six orders of noxious animals, which though so called are not parasites, but which have a special interest to stock-owners and veterinary practitioners, viz. Nematoda, Trematoda, Cestoda, Acanthocephala, Diptera, and Trachearia.—*Mr. W. S. Connochie, V.S., Selkirk, Ind. Agr.*, 19*th Dec.* 1885.—See Helminths.

Parrots. The tota or rose-ringed parrakeet rips up the ripe capsules of the poppy. If much disturbed, they steal suddenly down, cut off the capsule, which they carry to some adjoining tree. They are usually in small flocks, and if not watched they soon seriously reduce the seed produce of a field.

Paspalum scrobiculatum, *Linn.*, is sown in the end of June and cut in October. It suffers considerably from the attacks of insects, but is said to be protected from the ravages of birds by its ear being partially concealed in the leaf-sheath, as is the case with the coarse varieties of rice. Its use is liable to produce a sort of intoxication.—*D. & F.*—*Vern. Koda.*

Peenash, HIND. The larva of some insect takes up its abode in the cribriform plate of the ethmoid bone, and produces the disease known as the peenash in North-Western India. The larva is small, articulated, and terminates in a spiral tail ; its mouth and eyes are distinct.

Pellicularia koleroga, hypophylla, effusa, griseo-alba are fungi. Pellicularia koleroga, or black rot, or coffee-leaf rot, a fungus, an epiphyte which injures the leaves of the coffee tree.

Penicillaria spicata, *Willd.*, the bulrush millet, suffers still more than Sorghum vulgare from the microscopic fungus known to English farmers as ' bunt,' and in the North-Western Provinces is reported to be often infected with a species of mildew called ' bagulia ' (Puccinia, *sp.*), which manifests itself first in spots on the foliage, and then in total destruction of the grain. But it owes in great measure its liability to these diseases to the poverty of the soil on which it is cultivated, and the mildew is said to be most destructive in cases where it has been grown too frequently on the same land. Next to an absolute failure of rain, this millet suffers most from damp or rainy weather while it is in flower, by which the proper fertilization of the flowers is prevented. The stamens hang outside the flower-envelopes entirely unprotected from the weather, and it is perhaps to this that the Penicillaria owes its peculiar liability to damage from rain. If rain fall in the beginning of October, it is no uncommon thing to see a Penicillaria field with hardly a single grain formed on its spikes.—*D. & F.—Vern. Bajra.*

Periplaneta.—See Cockroach.

Phaseolus radiatus, *Linn.*, is the ' urd ' or ' mash.' If there be a long continuance of damp easterly winds, the plants suffer greatly from mildew.—*D. & F.—Vern. Urd, Mash.*

Phyllotreta nemorum, turnip-fly of Britain.

Phylloxera.—See Aphides.

Phymatea punctata aided in destroying the coffee industry of Ceylon.—See Cicadidæ ; Coffee Trees.

Physalia pelagica, the Portuguese man-o'-war, stings if handled, causing a good deal of irritation.—See Actineæ.

Pipsa, a troublesome dipterous insect which swarms

on the banks of the streams in Sikkim; it is very small, floating like a speck before the eye. The bite of the pipsa leaves a small spot of extravasated blood under the cuticle, very irritating if not opened. It resembles a flea, and is found on the banks of the Rungeet river in Sikkim. In 1883, an expedition was sent by the Indian Government against the Aka, a hill tribe whose territory lies to the north of Tezpur on the Brahmaputra. Both among troops and followers serious disability and loss of service resulted from the bite of this small insect.—See Eye-fly.

Pisum arvense, *Linn.,* and P. sativus, *Linn.,* are the field and garden peas. Like gram, they suffer (especially the white varieties) from frost, and from the ravages of the insect called ' bahādura.'—*D. & F.*—*Vern. Mattar, Batana.*

Poppy. The native cultivators engaged in the cultivation of the opium poppy distinguish several varieties which differ little in outward appearance, but considerably in the amount and quality of the opium they yield. In the North-Western Provinces, it is the white-flowered varieties that are grown for opium. In Malwa, the red or purple flowered kind is extensively cultivated. The insect enemies of the poppy are many, and have been arranged in three classes:—

1. Insects attacking the young poppy in November and December:—Acheta campestris, A. domesticus, and Acheta undetermined species; Grylli, two species; Gryllotalpa vulgaris.

2. Insects attacking the maturing poppy in February and March:—Mamestra papaverorum; Noctua, *sp.;* Bombyx, *sp.,* the buro bhooa; Gryllus, *sp.*

3. Insects which attack the poppy seeds in the

granaries:—Bruchus, *sp.*, larvæ and imago; Calandra, perfect insect; dipterous larvæ; Sitona, *sp.*; Tetranychus papaveræ; Tipula, *sp.*

The protection of the poppy plant is an object of great moment to the Government of British India, as will be recognised when it is mentioned that in the ten years 1875 to 1885 inclusive, the Indian revenue from opium averaged Rs. 9,47,10,229, or deducting the expenditure, an average net receipt of Rs. 7,20,30,816. In the year 1885–86, the value of the opium exported from India was Rs. 10,53,75,180.

In 1878, Mr. John Scott, writing from Deegah on the enemies of the poppy, reported that classes of moths appear there at two periods, one in February and March, when in their caterpillar state they are the foes of the young poppy; another class appearing in August, and disappearing in the early part of September, the caterpillar form of which feed chiefly on the young crops of the rainy seasons, legumes or pulses.

He recommended earlier sowings, rotation of crops, and on the appearance of the vernal insects, sprinkling the young plants in the evening with quicklime mixed with ashes or soot. Liberal irrigation, he says, brings the cricket and grasshopper class to the surface, where hand-picking and birds aid in their destruction.

In February and March 1871, the poppy crop in Behar was very seriously injured by heavy rain, accompanied by hail, and this was followed in March by blight of an unusually injurious character, under which the plant withered and turned black, and eventually died. The poppy in the Benares district became similarly diseased. The disease was attributed to the inclement weather. But in the south of the Patna district a grub lay concealed, burrowed in the ground all day, and at night came out and nipped off the young plant a little above the root, giving it the appearance of having been destroyed by hares. The blights of the poppy in Chota Nagpore are known as the lahai, moorka, and jureet. The lahai was that of 1871, which in Fyzabad was attributed to three insects called the ' gudarlah,' ' bhudo-weah,' and ' jewriah.' A winged insect appeared in Bustee called guduhilee, and two in Saharanpore, the ' koongy ' and ' mahoo.'

Among the diseases of the poppy crop enumerated by him are :—Aregma, broom-rapes, cladosporium, dactylium, gangrene, lecythea, mucor mucedo, orobranche, peronospora, petechiæ, phelipea, scleriasis, sporotrichum, sun-burning, trichoderma.

Scleriasis, a peculiar affection of the poppy, character-ized by the hardening, so to speak, of the whole outer tissues of the plant, and the utter arrest of the drug secretions. Such cases of functional derangement are very prevalent in the local crops from unselected seed, and subsequently cause serious deterioration to the crop. The disease or affection is hereditary ; that is, a large per-centage of the progeny is similarly affected. All plants so affected should be uprooted.

Petechiæ, another hereditary disease, is seriously deteriorative to the secretion of drug. All affected plants should be carefully removed.

Broom-rapes, the ' thokra ' of the natives, affect the roots of the poppy, etc. The seeds of these plants are so exceedingly minute that a breath of air will widely distribute them. The tomato and the brinjal (Solanum melongena) are affected by them. They should be care-fully uprooted on making their appearance.

Peronospora arborescens is a most serious parasitic foe of the opium poppy. It is a blight-mould confined to the leaves, and is more or less common on the plant in one or other of its modes of development. Differences in the degree of oxygenation of the juices promote, suppress, or impede the development of this mould.

Phelipea Indica, one of the broom-rapes, is a phœnogamic root parasite, frequently causing much damage to the poppy. Where it is of frequent occurrence, mustard seeds should be sown along with the poppy seeds. The growth of the poppy is not checked, but it never yields the full amount of opium. It is in many districts a serious pest to the poppy; is very prevalent in parts of the Patna Division. Orobranche cernua and O. Indica, two species of broom-rapes in Bengal, are parasites of the tobacco plant.

Sun - burning is the 'moorka' or 'joorka' of the natives, due to the sun scorching the plant. The leaves are dry and withered, with more or less discoloured purply-black or brownish veins. It occurs in hot seasons, with a deficiency of moisture in the soil.

Root canker occurs in stiff clayey soils, with an excess of the oxides of iron or manganese, or with an excess of any of the alkaline salts. The tap-root becomes corroded, and the leaves wither from below upwards.

Petechia. The leaves first acquire a pale yellow tinge, and subsequently the whole surface becomes gradually studded with specks and patches of a pale purply-black colour, but confined chiefly to the leaves. It is due to overcrowding in damp soils.

Gangrene occurs on all the affected plants; juices exude, forming small black specks, or even large black tears, all over the plant.

Dactylium roseum (*syn.* Tricothecium roseum), or thread-mould, is a creeping mycelium, from which arise short erect threads, crowned above with a few obovate, unistipitate spores. The mass is at first white, but at length acquires a pale rose colour. It occurs on various objects, living or dead, and is sometimes highly destructive to the cucumber plants. It is very common over all the poppy during moist warm weather, and also on opium everywhere, but does not injure the opium.

Trichoderma viride, a minute thread-mould, with snowy white threads, from which spring numerous spores of a pale greenish-yellow colour. It affects the roots and base of the stem of the poppy.

Sporotrichum, *sp.*, is not unfrequent on the roots of the poppy.

Cladosporium herbarium is very common in the older gummy exudations of the poppy, and on any injured part.

Mucor mucedo, an extremely common, blackish-looking mould.

Aregma moniliforme, the necklace brand, is found on the stem and leaves of the poppy.

Lecythea, *sp.*, is a yellow rust, which in 1866–67 formed a dense and thick layer over the surface of the leaves of the flax plant, Linum usitatissimum.

Trichobasis, *sp.*, an orange-coloured rust, is a parasitic fungus which causes extensive injury in the later cereal crops of Bengal, barley and wheat more especially. It also affects the tobacco and henbane plants.

Ustilago, *sp.*, is detected on the millets, or from the smut-coloured ears.

Caterpillars do some damage, and to attract them such crops as lettuce are sometimes mixed with the poppy.

An east wind during lancing time is exceedingly harmful, as the juice is prevented exuding properly. Dr. D. Cunningham, of the Bengal Medical Service, in 1875, published microscopical notes regarding the fungi present in opium blight.—*John Scott*, 1877.

Poppy seeds in the granary and store pots are injured by several insects :—Bruchus, two species, in their larval and perfect form ; Calandra, *sp.*, the perfect insect only ; dipterous larvæ ; Sitona, *sp.*, larva and perfect forms ; Tetranychus papaveræ, poppy seed mite ; Tipula, *sp.*, the larvæ and pupæ. The insects which attack the young poppy in November, December, February, and March are Acheta, three species ; Bombyx, *sp. ;* the Gryllus, two species, the kala-jhangha ; Gryllotalpa vulgaris ; Heliothes armigera ; and two species of Noctua.—*D. & F.—Vern. Posta.*—See Fungi.

Porcupine.—See Mammalia.

Prionus, a genus of the longicornes or capricorn beetles. They inhabit the plants of an Alpine region.—*R. T.*

Pseudococcus adonidum, the mealy bug of Ceylon coffee-planters.

Puccinia graminis, the corn mildew fungus.

Pulex, the flea genus. P. canis, P. felis, P. gallinæ, P. meles are the fleas of the dog, lion, fowl, and badger. Fleas are numerous even on the sea-shores of the cool climate of Great Britain in the hot weather. But in tropical countries, in warehouses and other buildings where no diet for them seems to exist, they are occasionally in myriads. Mr. W. M. Williams, writing in *Science Gossip*, December 1884, says he had found fleas in limestone caverns, where their only possible supply of food was the animal matter that may have remained in the fossils, of which the limestone was chiefly composed. They appear in countless numbers in India, almost everywhere, at the closing months of the year, alike in the most exposed as in the most sheltered spots, and the most bare and rocky ground.

R

Reptile pests of India are noticed under Crocodiles and Snakes. The toad is serviceable in the kitchen garden as a slug and insect destroyer, but it is a determined bee-eater. The honey-laden bees returning from their foraging may fall at the bottom of their hive and become the prey of the watchful toad.

Rhynchites, a genus of small weevils, very destructive of the forests of Northern India. By it and the species of Bruchus, in 1863, entire seed crops of the Shorea robusta were destroyed.

Rhynchophora, or the weevil family, of the order Coleoptera. Its most destructive genera are Bruchus, Calandra, Curculio, and Rhyncoenus.

Rhynchophorus palmarum attacks the palms, bananas, and sugar-cane in Malacca.

Rhyncoenus, a genus of the rhynchophora or weevil family.—*R. T.*

Rice is the food of the well-to-do classes along the coasts and in the valleys of British India. Rice, in the North-Western Provinces, has most to fear from the 'green fly,' called 'gandiki' or 'tank;' and as they do not commence their attacks until towards the end of August, it is the finer varieties which suffer most. Strong and healthy plants suffer much less than backward ones; and this is a reason for early sowing.—*D. & F.— Vern. Dhan.*—See **Paraponyx.**

Ricinus communis, *Linn.,* the castor - oil plants, when allowed to stand three or four years in the North-Western Provinces, become breeding - ground for a hairy brown caterpillar, which is supposed to bring ill-luck.—*D. & F.* —*Vern. Arendi.*

Rust is a disease of plants. Peridermium Thomsonii, *Berk.,* affects the foliage and twigs of coniferous trees of Northern India and Himalaya. Other known species are Periderm. pini, *Chev.,* Europe; P. elatinum, *Link.,* Europe; and P. columni. Leaf rusts are also known to be caused by Melampsora salicina; M. populina, *Lev.;* M. Tremulæ, *Lev.;* M. betulina, *Desm.;* M. padi, *Kurze.;* Uredo quercus; Lecythea mixta, *Lev.;* L. saliceti, *Lev.;* Puccinia prunorum; P. buxi, *D.;* Uromyces buxi, *Cooke,* Himalaya.

S

Saccharum officinarum, *Linn.,* is the sugar-cane. Many varieties of it are grown in India, but they may be noticed here as edible and non-edible cane, the former being eaten raw, as a fruit, while the latter is utilized in the manufacture of sugar. Edible cane is much the thicker, softer, and juicier, and is grown with very high cultivation. Its principal variety is in the North-Western Provinces known as the 'phaunda.' In the North-Western Provinces the most distinct varieties of non-edible cane are four in number, viz. the 'dikchan' of Rohilkhand, called 'barokha' in Cawnpore, growing as high as 10 feet; one of 5 or 6 feet, called 'agholi' or 'matna;' thirdly, a hard, tall, reddish cane, of poor quality, called 'chin,' and grown without irrigation in damp localities; and fourth, the 'dhor,' a dwarf cane, white and hard. Sugar-cane is propagated by layers or cuttings, long enough to include two internodes, *i.e.* two nodes or joints. The young canes are produced from buds, which spring from the nodes under artificial stimulation, by burying them for several days in damp earth, and soaking in water for twelve hours before planting. In Bareilly, an ordinary plough, which has been appeased with sacrificial offerings of turmeric and rice, and decorated with the 'tika' in red earth, strikes the first furrow. This is followed in the same furrow by a second, with mould-board attached to widen and deepen the furrow. Behind this comes the sower, wearing silver ornaments, with a necklace of flowers round his neck and a red tika on his forehead. He is usually fed with ghi and sweetmeats before commencing. He is called the hathi or elephant. He throws the bits of cane into the furrow immediately behind the second plough, at intervals of about a foot. Behind the elephant comes a second man, called the kawa or crow, who picks up the bits that have not fallen into the furrow, and puts them in properly ; and occasionally the gudha or donkey, a third man, accompanies the elephant, carrying a basket of cuttings, which he supplies as needed.

Sugar-cane, in the North-Western Provinces, suffers at times from the attacks of caterpillars, one of them, called 'kanswa' in the Meerut district, attacking the young shoots, and another, the 'silai,' the full-grown plants. The most serious injury to cane grown on low lands results from being flooded in the rainy season. It is a costly plant to grow, occupying the ground for many months, requiring a rich soil, abundant manure, and careful irrigation. *The Animal Parasites of the Sugar-cane,* by H. Ling Roth (London, Trübner & Co., 1885), says a species of Hoplosternus is the common chafer of Queensland. Its grub destroys the roots of the sugar-cane, causing the leaves to become brown and dry up; the growth of the cane is thus arrested, and the first high wind knocks its over. In this manner whole fields of cane are killed. In the early stage, the larvæ are occupied in gnawing the root. In November and December, the chafers, fully developed, appear above ground in swarms, remaining inactive during the day, but feeding eagerly at night. An ant, the Formica saccharivora, is supposed to get at the sweet juices of this plant. The waxy sugar-cane louse, known to the Mauritius and Bourbon planters as Le pou à poche blanche, is the Icerya sacchari. It occurs in Queensland, and Mr. Roth supposes that it is milked by a small black ant, Formica rufonigra, in the same manner as species of Aphides are milked by other ants. He considers it to be a cause of injury to the cane. The sugar-cane beetle of the United States is the Ligyrus ruficeps, *Le C.* It is a stout black beetle, half an inch long, which bores into the stalk of the sugar-cane under ground. Sugar-cane ravages in Grenada are caused by the cane spittle-fly, Delphax saccharivora; in Natal, by the cane smut, Ustilago sacchari, a disease analagous to the smut of wheat and maize; in the Mauritius, by the Proceras sacchariphagus, which Mr. Westwood has supposed may be identical with the Diatræa sacchari, *Guilding,* and Phalæna sacchari, *Fabricius.* The 'borer' of the Queensland cane has been supposed to be the larva of this Diatræa sacchari. It enters the cane above ground, and eats up the heart. It is believed to be identical with the borer of the Mauritius, the Proceras sacchariphagus.

The wire-worm, larvæ of the click-beetle, are to be

found at the roots of the Queensland cane, but no damage from them has been detected. W. Bancroft, writing in 1878, says that he had with advantage sown the Dolichos lablab and Cajanus Indicus amongst and around sugar-cane fields to attract the ichneumon flies which destroyed the louse.—*D. & F.—Vern. Ikh, Ghanna.*

Salamandra maculata, the terrestrial salamander, secretes a poisonous milky fluid. The aqueous salamander is Triton cristatus.

Sand-fly, a pest of Kurdistan, a serious torment, penetrating through everything, and preventing sleep.—*Rich.*

Saperda, *sp.,* a longicorn beetle, found in the forests of the North-Western Provinces.—*R. T.*

Sarcoptidæ, a family of the Arachnoidea, comprising the itch and louse mites in the genera Sarcoptes, Psoroptes, Symbiotes, Myobia, Listiophorus, Myocoptes, Dermaleichus, and Demodex. They infest the smaller mammals.

The itch insect, Sarcoptes scabiei, is extremely minute, so that it is only just visible to the naked eye; it is ·012 of an inch in length, and ·009 of an inch in breadth. They can tunnel their way with considerable speed. M. Bourguignon considers that one of these insects could travel from the hand to the shoulder in less than ten minutes. Other species occur in the lower animals, but most animals have their own peculiar parasites, and species can be transferred. Sulphur, petroleum, kerosene, and copaiva kill them.

Saw-flies.—See Tenthredo.

Schizodactylus monstrosus, *Westwood.* A leviathan mole-cricket, which abounds in Monghir indigo fields. It is called jhengur in Hindi.

Sclerostoma syngamus are worms which lodge in the trachea of fowls, and cause the gapes.

Scolopendridæ. Myriapods or Centipedes occur in India 10 inches long. Mecistocephalus punctifrons is a species of the East Indies. Scolopendra Ceylonensis is of that island; Sc. tuberculidens is of the East Indies; Sc. cœrulio-viridis is of Australia, as also is Cremata Smithii. Geophelus Cummingii occurs in the Philippines.—*M. T.*

Scolytus, a genus of the Xylophagi.

Scorpions. The true scorpions belong to the sub-family Scorpiones, one of the Arachnoidea, and include the Buthus afer, B. Cæsar of the East Indies, and B. imperator (locality doubtful). Androctonus priamus occurs in Java, and species of Androctonus in Rangoon and other parts of the East Indies. With the scorpion when about to strike, an exceedingly minute drop of the poison is seen to exude at the extremity of the spine, the discharge taking place before this is introduced into the flesh of the victim; but the secretion becomes more abundant when the point meets with the resisting body (*Blanchard*). The poison is expelled by the contraction of the surrounding muscular fibres.—*M. T.*

Scorpion beetle, Anthia sexguttata.

Sesamum Indicum, *Linn.* The til in the North-Western Provinces is liable to damage from ill-timed rain.—*Vern. Til.—D. & F.*

Setaria italica, *Beauv,* is sown at the commencement of the rains, and reaped in September. Great loss is sustained by the depredations of birds.—*Vern. Kangni.—D. & F.*

Silk is produced by several genera of the Bombycidæ, called silk-worms. Silk-worms are liable to several diseases. Luisettes are worms which have not strength to moult. They should be early removed, as they die and infect the room. Arpians have exhausted all their strength in the last moult, and have not even strength to eat.

Yellow or flat worms easily die. The flat or mous are soft and indolent worms, become very fat from eating a great deal, and soon die and become putrid.

The most severe disease, as the most general, is the muscadine. A worm may be eating as usual, when suddenly it becomes a dull white, and not long after dies, becoming reddish and rigid. Twenty-four hours after death a white efflorescence shows itself round the head and rings, and soon after all the body becomes floury. This flour is a fungus, the Botrytis bassiana, of which the mycelium develops itself in the fatty tissue of the caterpillar, attacks the intestines, and fructifies in the exterior. Some suppose this disease to be contagious.

The Gattine ailment is an epidemic disease which shows itself from the very beginning of the rearing. The losses it occasions in Europe are very great. The domesticated silk-worms in India are greatly diseased.

Sitona. A beetle which attacks the stored poppy seed, rice, maize, wheat, barley, and the millets. It is one of the most destructive of the many kinds of insects which affect the granaries of India ; it is about an eighth of an inch long, of a pale chestnut brown colour. The larva forms and perfect forms are alike destructive.— *J. Scott.*

Sitophilus oryzæ, the common rice-weevil of India.

Snakes, in natural history, are placed in the class Reptilia, and order Ophidia. They are numerous in the East Indies and in the Eastern seas. All the sea-snakes are poisonous, and dreaded by fishermen. They are classed by naturalists as the Hydrophidæ, and comprise the genera Acalyptus, Aipysurus, Disteria, Enhydrina,

Hydrophis, Pelamis, and Platurus. The land snakes are greatly the more numerous, but there are not many of them poisonous,—genera Bungarus, Callophis, Daboia, Megærophis, Naja, Ophiophagus, and Xenurelaps. In India, in 1884–85, 19,629 persons and 1728 cattle died from snake-bites, and Government gave Rs. 28,551 in rewards for killing 380,981 poisonous snakes. These rewards are the only means had recourse to by the British Indian Government to destroy snakes. But the people might be encouraged to keep fowls, and particularly the guinea-fowl, to destroy the eggs and young snakes. Snake-birds and the mongoose are their natural enemies. Earth, the ligature, and the knife are the means always at hand to remedy the bites of venomous snakes. Some of the pythons of India are 16 to 24 feet long. Snakes are said to avoid the fennel plant, Nigella sativa, as well as all places strewed with fennel seed.

Solpurgidæ, a family of the class Arachnoidea. Galeodes araneoides, one of this family, is a great spider of the Central Asia steppes. It moves abroad at night, to seize and eat all weaker creatures, as lizards, bats, and musk rats. Galeodes fatalis has been known to kill a sparrow, and they even eat their own species. Thirty to thirty-five of this genus are known to naturalists.

Sorghum vulgare, *Pers.*, is the cholum or juari of India. The most peculiar of the diseases to which it is liable is that which makes the young stalks poisonous to cattle, if eaten by them when semi-parched from want of rain. Of the fact there can be no doubt; in the scarcity of 1877 large numbers of cattle were known to perish from this cause, their bodies becoming inflated after a meal of the young juár plants, and death ensuing shortly afterwards, apparently in severe pain. A good explanation is not, however, forthcoming. The opinion universally accepted by natives is, that young juár when suffering from deficiency of rain becomes infested with an insect called 'bhaunri,' to which its poisonous effect on cattle is due. Immediately rain falls the insect is said to perish, and unless the ears have appeared before the rain failed, the crop often recovers itself and yields a good out-turn of grain. Juár is peculiarly liable to a species of bunt (Tilletia), a parasitic fungus well known in English corn-fields, which converts the whole contents of grains, externally apparently perfectly healthy, into a foul, greasy, dark-coloured powder. But birds and squirrels are probably the worst enemies the cultivator has to contend with, and their depredations necessitate the crops being watched for at least twenty-five days before it is cut, which adds, of course, to the cost of cultivation.—*J. F. D.; W. B. F.*

Sphænophorus planipennis, weevil of Ceylon, attacks the palms.

Spiders.—See Araneidæ.

Squirrel.—See Mammalia.

Starling. The rose-coloured starling, Pastor roseus, *Linn.,* is a famous locust killer, but their flocks commit immense depredations on the white sorghum and the mulberry. The pied starling is Sturnopastor contra.

Sternocera chrysis, the rose beetle.

Stomoxys calcitrans has a hard, sharp-pointed proboscis, which pierces thick knickerbocker stockings, and inflicts a sharp sting.—*Capt. St. John.*

Strongylus filaria is a small round thread-worm of a yellowish-white colour, from 1 to $2\frac{1}{2}$ inches long. They are found in the air passages and lung tissue of lambs and young sheep, and cause the serious and destructive

' lamb disease.' Another species of a similar appearance, the Strongylus micrurus, is the cause of the disease in calves and young cattle termed ' hoose ' or ' husk,' from the animal suffering from them being subject to violent and convulsive fits of coughing. It is often fatal to calves. The pig is also infested with a similar worm, which is named Strongylus suis. A fourth species, the Strongylus contortus, is a habitant of the fourth stomach of the sheep and goat, and is the cause of the disease termed ' parasitic gastric [catarrh.' A fifth species, Strongylus armatus, affects the horse's stomach. It is now believed that the ova of these parasites, after passing from the body of their host, retain their vitality in damp places only, and that nice bites of green grass, such as that growing on the sides of open drains, and damp spots on pastures otherwise dry, are sources of danger, as the parasitic ova infest such grasses.—*The India Agriculturist.*—See Helminths.

Sugar, unclarified, or gur. Gur is an article of general consumption. There is perhaps no article of food which is so profitable to the storer, but at the same time the storage is accompanied by great risks. There is great danger from wasps and hornets, and heat causes the gur to melt. To guard against these dangers, the gur is buried in bhusa (bran). Each pari (a large cake, average one and a half maunds weight) is placed in the sun, cut in two and dried, and again cut and dried, so that each pari is made into four pieces. These pieces are laid in a store-room on narkul matting spread over a layer of bhusa. The pieces are kept a little apart. Over them is thrown bhusa, and the sides closed in with tat. Sometimes a large sheet of coarse cloth (chandni) is used to cover the heap.

T

Tacua speciosa, a native of Java, one of the Cicadidæ, is black, and 3 inches in length.—See Cicadidæ.

Tænia solium, *Linn.* This species, which is familiarly known as the solitary or tape worm, is a very common entozoon. There are several species.—See Helminths.

Tarantula spiders are popularly believed to be exceedingly poisonous. These animals belong to the genus Lycosa of Latreille; they are characterized by having the eyes arranged in an elongated quadrilateral form. There are several species.

Tea-bug or mosquito blight of Assam is the Helopeltis theiovora. Other species of this genus are H. nigra and H. braconiformis of New Guinea and Waigiou; H. pellucida and H. collaris of the Philippines; H. podagrica, of some unascertained habitat. H. Antonii attacks the cacao plants in Ceylon; H. Bradyi does much mischief to the cinchona plantations in Java; and another species (not yet described) injures the tea plants also in Java.

The Tea-mite or red spider of Assam planters is the Tetranychus bioculatus.

Mr. Wood-Mason, writing in 1884, remarks that ' of the numerous animals which prey upon the tea plant, two only are at present known to do such injury to it as materially to diminish the profits of owners of tea estates ; these are the Tea-Bug or " Mosquito Blight," and the Tea-Mite or " Red Spider " of planters.' The former damages the young and tender shoots required for manufacture into tea, and thus causes direct loss to the planter ; while the latter confines its ravages to the full-grown leaves, and by so injuring these organs as to unfit them for the performance of their important functions, checks the growth of green shoots, prevents the bushes from flushing, and thus inflicts upon him indirect loss. Both the mite and the bug pass their whole lives on the tea plant, and neither has been met with on any other plant. Yet the tea-bug, known as the mosquito blight, has been supposed to find shelter in the toon trees, planted along the roads of the tea-gardens. Wherever there are toon trees, the mosquito blight is said to prevail; and the most severely attacked tea bushes are said to be those near the toon (Cedrela toona).

Mr. R. Thompson mentions that a beetle deposits eggs into the main stem of the tea plant at the root, and the larva, so soon as hatched, bores into the pith and then works up or down, the tunnel being of a size to ultimately kill the plant. The larva undergoes the pupa change in the tunnel near the root.

A tea blight caused by the attacks of acari on the tea plants, as also of other wingless insects, is said to be prevented by planting hemp (Cannabis sativa).—*R. T.*

Tenthredo. The saw-flies and their caterpillars never attack wood, but live entirely on leaves, though the perfect insects are known to lay their eggs in the bark of trees.—*R. T.*

Termites, or white ants, species of the insect family Termitidæ, do enormous mischief. Their attacks are indiscriminate on all wooden, woollen, cotton, or paper articles; rarely growing plants, though the sugar-cane is often injured by them; and as they form galleries in their destructive advances, their ravages are often undiscovered, however much they may be watched. The queen will lay 80,000 eggs in a day, for a long time. Many

THE AGRICULTURAL PESTS OF INDIA.

valuable buildings in which wood forms a part are damaged by them. Teak-wood is not attacked. Their nests are raised about 3 or 4 feet in height above ground, brought up from below as they form the galleries. These nests largely harbour the poisonous cobra, and are sites for the serpent-worship of the Hindoos.

Tetranichidæ, the spinning mites, a section of the class Arachnoidea. Its genus Tetranychus has many species, and one of them, T. papaveræ, the poppy seed mite, is an enemy of the poppy. T. telarius is the red spider. Tetranychus papaveræ, one of the Trombidina, attacks in swarms the poppy seed in the granaries and store pots, reducing it to chaff and dust, and their excreta glueing the seed together in pellets more or less bulky. It looks like a minute spider, being not more than a line in length, shining, and of a rich claret colour. It multiplies with great rapidity. A little powdered camphor sprinkled among the store pots is an effectual preventive of this pest, which, with species of Bruchus, Calandra, Sitona, and Tipula, are the chief depredators on the poppy seed store pots in Lower Bengal. Tetranychus bioculatus is the tea-mite or red spider of Assam planters.—*J. Scott.*—See Tea-bug.

Thrips adonidum, a small hemipterous insect, which, like other members of this order, is provided with a beak or rostrum specially adapted for piercing and sucking and feeding on the juices of the leaves and softer parts of plants. It punctures and destroys the whole surface of the poppy leaf. It is one of the many kinds of minute insects which the natives of Northern India called Lhi. Their black glutinous excreta, voided on the leaf of the poppy, suppress respiration, and the whole leaf dries up and withers. It destroys the seed produce of the poppy, but in no way impairs the returns of opium extract.   It is more abundant in hot, dry seasons.—*J. Scott.*

Thypa eucharis attacks the Calotropis gigantea.

Tineidæ.   A group of Micro-Lepidoptera, comprising a large number of species.   Some of them feed upon vegetable substances; some live in the stalks of plants, corn, etc.; others mine the surface of the leaves, or live between the surfaces of leaves.   Many of the species form galleries or moveable cases out of the materials upon which they feed.   Some species feed on feathers, hair, or dry animal matter.   The clothes moths belong to this family.   Some species of Galleria live in bees' nests, and occasionally do much mischief.

Tipula.   Species of tipula are known as the crane-fly or daddy long-legs.   The larvæ hatched from their eggs feed on the tender rootlets of grass and other herbage, and also attack young plants.   They often do an immense amount of mischief, laying bare large patches of meadow, and destroying great quantities of young corn.   The caterpillar of one Bengal species, in 1878, was a very serious enemy of the young poppy, eating it off during the night.   It is three-quarters of an inch long, appearing in December to the middle of January, when they bury themselves in the soil and change to pupæ, the perfect insect appearing in February and March.   Nothing but hand-picking was found of use.   The head of the larva is black and horny, with keenly incisive jaws, the body colour varies from clayey-brown to greyish-black. Tipula larvæ do much injury to the stored poppy seed, but can be prevented by sprinkling powdered camphor in the pots and granaries.—*R. T.; J. S.*

Tomici.   The species of the genera Hylesinus, Scolytus, and Tomicus are small beetles, but numerous and common.

Tomici chiefly affect bamboos, and are very destructive to them. The Hylesini also attack the bamboo, but not so vigorously as their smaller brethren the Tomici, and both are detected by the powdery excremented matter which they and their larvæ throw out. One small species of Hylesinus in great numbers attacks the dead wood of the cheer pine, and when hatched underneath the bark, they bore in all directions, the tendency, however, being to reach the centre of the log. They do not attack living trees, nor logs that have had their bark stripped off. Tomicus perforans, monographus, in 1860, attacked the beer barrels in the commissariat stores of Burma and Lower Bengal, and the contents oozed out from a multitude of pores, causing great loss. The soldiers gave the insect an apt name — they called it Tippling Tommy. Tomici greatly affect bamboos.—*R. T.*

Trap-door spiders comprise species of the genera Atypus, Cteniza, Mygale, of the tribe Mygalidæ and order Araneidæ.

Trichina spiralis, *Owen,* a nematoid parasite, has its seat in the muscular system of the human race. They may exist in such numbers as to defy enumeration, yet their presence does not seem in the least to impair the functions of the part in which they are embedded; and similarly, as mentioned by Professor Williams, sheep have been killed in prime condition by the butcher, and their lungs found loaded with filaria. A female may have 10,000 to 15,000 embryo. They have not yet been detected in India.—*J. S. of Arts,* 14, 21*st July* 1871.

Triticum sativum, *Linn.* Wheat. Indian, like English wheat, suffers from the attacks of microscopic fungi, but not to the same extent, owing doubtless to the greater dryness of the climate. There is, however, a considerable difference in this respect between one locality and another. In the Meerut and Rohilkhand Divisions, where winter rains are of regular occurrence, and dense mists often prevail in December and January, it would be difficult to find a wheat-field in which some plants were not attacked by rust, and occasionally considerable damage is suffered from it; while in the centre and south of the North-Western Provinces it often requires a considerable amount of searching in order to discover such specimens. The commonest of the fungus disease to which wheat is liable is the one known as 'rattua' or 'girwi,' which appears to be identical with the English mildew or rust. The plant tissues become filled with minute orange-coloured spores, which when ripe burst through the plant skin in longitudinal fissures, sprinkling the leaves and ears with a reddish powder. In this condition it is known to botanists under the generic name of Trichobasis, from the fact that each spore is furnished with a short hair-like protrusion or stalk. As the plant ripens, clusters of minute bodies appear, each consisting of a stalk fixed in the leaf tissues, bearing a double-celled head. These bodies grow out in clusters, each cluster appearing to the naked eye a minute black spot. In this stage the fungus is known as Puccinia, and was long supposed to be a separate plant from the Trichobasis, instead of merely a stage in its history.

When ears of wheat are distorted and thickly covered with a dark brown or black dust, the plant is infected with the disease known to English farmers as 'smut' (Ustilago), and to natives as 'kandwa.' The dust is composed of very minute globular spores far smaller than those of Trichobasis, but resembling them in being single celled. Rust does not necessarily altogether destroy the produce, although it almost invariably deteriorates it; but nothing survives the attacks of smut. The name 'kandwa' is applied to a totally distinct disease in the case of the millets, when it denotes the fungus known as 'bunt' or 'ergot' in England, which fills the grain with a greasy black powder, leaving the plant, and indeed the grain itself, externally perfectly healthy looking. Bunt does not appear to be so common in wheat in Hindustan as in England.

The disease known as 'lakhua' (Polycystis) consists of spores which fill the plant tissues, and break out when ripe in longitudinal fissures exactly like rust, from which, however, it differs, in each spore bëing a spherical agglomeration of numerous cells (somewhat resembling a blackberry in shape), instead of being unicellular. Lakhua is said altogether to prevent a plant from bearing ears.

But by far the most extraordinary disease to which wheat is liable is that known as 'sehwan,' in which the young wheat grains are found to be filled with minute worms in various stages of development, comparatively large sized (apparently), males and females being associated with a mass of oval-shaped eggs, from which smaller and less highly organized worms emerge. As the grain ripens at harvest-time, these worms will be found to have completely filled the grain, having entirely ousted (and possibly eaten) the males, females, and eggcases to which they owe their origin. The grain is much shrivelled, and of a dark colour, and can be easily recognised as infected. The most extraordinary fact connected with this disease is, however, that the worms can retain their vitality for a very long time, although unprovided with any source of nutriment; and if an

infected grain is examined a year after harvest, they will
be found matted together in an entangled mass, apparently torpid, but showing no signs of death or decay.
This would seem to indicate that their life in the wheat
grain is only one chapter of their history.

The worms have since been identified as belonging to
the order Nematoidea, and are apparently of the genus
Tylenchus.   They issue from the infected grain when
sown, and attack the growing corn, gaining admission
into the flowers, when as yet undeveloped, preventing the
development of the grain, and producing in its place a
green gall (mistaken for the grain above) in which they
reside.— *Vern. Gandum, Gehun.*—*D. & F.*

Trombidiidæ.   Species of this section attack in swarms
the poppy seed in the granaries and store pots, reducing
it to chaff and dust, and their excreta gluing the seed
together in pellets more or less bulky.   It looks like a
minute spider, being not more than a line in length,
shiny, and of a rich claret colour.   It multiplies with
great rapidity.   A little powdered camphor sprinkled
among the store pots is an effectual preventive.—*J. Scott.*
—See Acarina, Tetranichidæ.

U

Uredo segetum, a parasitic fungus, known as 'smut.'

Ustilago sacchari, sugar-cane smut, of Natal, an
analagous disease to the smut of wheat and maize.

V

Vespidæ.   The family of hymenopterous insects commonly known as wasps.   The principal genera are Vespa,

555

Polistes, Polybia. An Indian hornet (Vespa crabroniformis) builds a nest of great size. One of India's boldest birds, the myna, flees before the hornet's threatened attacks. The Formica smaragdina, an ant of all India, is said to drive off the wasps.

W

Wasp.—See Vespidæ.
Weevil.—See Curculionidæ.
White Ants.—See Termites.
Wood-borer.—See Borer.

X

Xylocopa, or carpenter bees, bore tunnels in timber, where they collect honey and the farina of flowers, leaving a lump of the compound in a divided cell for the nourishment of the young larva when it is hatched. Each cell has, with the egg, a separate supply of food. The larvæ are sub-cylindrical, whitish worms. They undergo the pupa state within their respective cells, and come out the perfect bee after a brief period. The largest species is X. purpurea, the bhoura; it is a strong-flighted, active insect, very destructive to the wood of buildings, and also to the dead wood of forest trees. One of them, at the Kurnool hospital, was seen to strike a sparrow dead.

Xylophagi. A group of Rhynchophorus Coleoptera, containing a large number of wood-boring species. The principal genera are Tomicus, Hylesinus, Scolytus, and Platypus.

Xylotrechus.—See Coffee-borer.

Xylotrupes gideon attacks the cocoa-nut trees in Malacca.

Z

Zea mays, *Linn.*, in the North-Western Provinces is singularly free from disease of any kind, and the only insect from which it suffers is a small caterpillar, called ' salai ' or 'silai,' which burrows in the stalk and leaf-sheaths. On the other hand, it is more liable than any other crop to the depredations of parrots, squirrels, wild hog, jackals, porcupines, and thieves; and at least for a fortnight before harvest-time some member of the cultivator's family has to watch the crop from a tall platform in the centre of the field, armed with a sling or catapult or thong, and shouting to scare the marauders. Maize is a very exhausting crop.—*D. & F.*—*Vern. Muka juari.*

Zeuzeridæ, a family of moths. Their caterpillars feed in the wood of the inside of the trunks of trees.—See Coffee.

INDEX.

ABLAQ MYNA, Hind., Sturnopastor contra, v. Caterpillars, Starling.
Acarus coffeæ, an enemy of the coffee plant of Ceylon, r. Coffee.
Acarus telarius, syn. of Gamasus telarius, q.v.
Actinopus, genus of Mygalidæ, v. Araneidæ.
Adolia, sp., v. Caterpillars.
Alligators, v. Crocodiles.
Aloa lactinea, Cram., one of the Lepidoptera of Ceylon; it injures the coffee plant, v. Coffee.
Alopecia, v. Fungi.
Ancylonicha, sp., White grub, v. Coffee, Melolonthidæ.
Ancylostomum duodinale, a worm of the order Nematoda, r. Helminths.
Anomala elata, its grub injures the coffee plant in Ceylon, v. Coffee, Coleoptera.
Anthomyza coffeæ, v. Coffee.
Anthophora, a genus of the Apidæ, q.v.
Anthrax, v. Mammals.
Ant lion, v. Myrmeleon.
Apathus, a genus of the Apidæ, q.v.
Arachnoidea, v. Araneidæ.
Arachnothera, v. Araneidæ.
Aræocerus coffeæ, a beetle of the family Anthribidæ, order Coleoptera. It does much injury to many seeds, including coffee beans. It is cosmopolitan, v. Coffee, Coleoptera.
Arceuthobium oxycedri, v. Parasites.
Arctia, v. Gossypium, Alope.
Aregma, necklace brand poppy disease, v. Poppy.
Aromatic herbs are protective, v. p. 18.

Ascaris. Intestinal worm of the order Nematoda, v. Helminths.
Atypus, trap-door spider, genus of Mygale, v. Araneidæ, Trap - door Spiders.

BAGULIA, Hind., Puccinia, sp., v. Penicillaria.
Bahadura, Hind., caterpillar ravages Cicer arietinum, q.v., also Pisum arvense.
Balistes, a genus of poisonous fish, v. Fish.
Barley, Hordeum vulgare, q.v.
Bean-beetle, Bruchus granarius, v. Bruchus.
Bhooa or Buro-Bhoo, Hind., a species of Bombyx, v. p. 31.
Bhoura, Xylocopa, sp., q.v.
Bhudoweah, Hind., insect, v. Poppy.
Blabera, sp., Cockroach, q.v.
Black bug, Lecanium nigrum, v. Bug, Coffee.
Black grub, Agrotis segetum, q.v.
Black-leg, v. Mammals.
Black rot, Pellicularia, sp., q.v.
Blatta orientalis, Cockroach, q.v.
Blue-bottle fly, v. Flies, Muscidæ.
Boarmia, sp., v. Caterpillars, Coffee.
Boat-fly, Notonecta glauca, v. Bug.
Boletus, a fungus, v. Fungi.
Bombus, a genus of the Apidæ, q.v.
Bothriocephalus latus, a helminth of the order Cestoda, v. Helminths.
Botrytis, a fungus, v. Fungi, Silk.
Broom-rapes, a poppy disease, v. Poppy.
Buffaloes injured by a Bombyx, q.v.
Bug of Miana, Argas Persicus, v. Argades.

Cteniza, genus of Mygalidæ, trap-door spider, *v.* Araneidæ.
Cumbly poochie, Tam., *v.* Alope.
Curculio attack cocoa-nut trees, *v.* Cocoa-nut Palm.
Curculionidæ. The larvæ of the Buprestidæ and Elateridæ feed on living wood, *v.* Coleoptera.
Curuminga beetle, Batocera ruber, *q.v.*
Cyanea, *v.* Actinia.
Cysticercus cellulosa, larva of Tænia communis; C. acanthotrocus, larva of Tænia acanthotrias, *v.* Helminths.

DABREE TREE of Kamaon, host of an aphis, *v.* Aphidæ.
Dactylium roseum, thread-mould poppy disease, a creeping mycelium, *v.* Poppy.
Dadap tree, Erythrina Indica, *q.v.*
Daddy long-legs, Tipula, *sp.*, *q.v.*
Danais chrysippus. It is largely mimicked, *v.* Butterflies.
Death-watch, Anobium, *v.* Bookworm.
Demodex, *v.* Sarcoptidæ.
Dermaleichus, *v.* Sarcoptidæ.
Dimya, *v.* Ants.
Diodon tigrina, a poisonous fish, *v.* Fish.
Diplodia, *v.* Fungi.
Diplosis tritici, American wheat midge, *v.* p. 15.
Distoma, genus of helminths, of the order Trematoda, *v.* Helminths.
Distylium racemosum, *v.* Aphidæ.
Dothidea, *v.* Fungi.
Dragon flies, *v.* Culex, Flies.
Drepana, *sp.*, *v.* Caterpillars, Coffee.
Dysgoniidæ, a moth family, *v.* Achæa.
Dyticidæ, the water-beetle family of the Coleoptera; they are carnivorous, *v.* Coleoptera.

ECHINOCOCCUS HOMINIS, larva of Tænia dentalis, *v.* Helminths.
Echinococcus veterinorum, larva of Tænia echinococcus, *v.* Mammals.
Englossa, genus of the Apidæ, *q.v.*
Ephemeridæ, *v.* Flies.
Epizootic aphtha, *v.* Foot-and-mouth disease, Mammals.
Ergot, *v.* Fungi, Triticum.

Euchirus, *v.* Palm trees, Lamellicornes.
Eupithecia coffearia, *v.* Caterpillars, Coffee.
Euproctis viguncula, *Walker*, one of the Lepidoptera, attacks the coffee plant in Ceylon, *v.* Caterpillars.
Eurotium, *v.* Fungi.

FAVUS, *v.* Fungi.
Festucaria lentis, a helminth of the order Trematoda, *v.* Helminths.
Fish-insect, Lepisma, *sp.*, *v.* Bookworm.
Fly, *v.* Cecidomyia.
Foot-and-mouth disease, or Aphtha epizootica, *v.* Mammals.
Forest enemies, *v.* Batocera, Bruchus Bug, Buprestis, Coleoptera, Capnodium mangiferum, Ceriosterna gladiator.
Formica, *v.* Ants, Aphidæ, Honeydew, Icerya, Saccharum, Vespidæ.
Frost ruins growing Cajanus Indicus and Cicer arietinum, *q.v.*

GALEOPITHECUS VOLANS, Flying lemur, *v.* Flying Fox.
Galleriomorpha lichenoides, *Feld.*, *v.* Coffee.
Gall-insect, *v.* Cynips, Hymenoptera.
Galls, *v.* Aphidæ.
Gamasidæ, *v.* Acarina.
Gandiki, *v.* Rice.
Ganja, flower head of Cannabis, *q.v.*
Gapes, *v.* Sclerostoma syngamus.
Gavialidæ, *v.* Crocodiles.
Geocores, family of Hemiptera, *v.* Cimicidæ, Bug.
Girwi fungus, *v.* Triticum.
Glenospora, *v.* Fungi.
Gnat, *v.* Culex.
Goats injured by a Bombyx, *q.v.*
Gobius criniger, Bay of Bengal, poisonous, *v.* Fish.
Goorgooria, Hind., Gryllotalpa vulgaris, *q.v.*
Green fly, *v.* Rice.
Grub, *v.* Agrotis segetum.
Gudarlah insect, *v.* Poppy.
Gur, *v.* Sugar.

HALACARIDÆ, *v.* Acarina.
Halictus, genus of the Apidæ, *q.v.*

www.ingramcontent.com/pod-product-compliance
Lightning Source LLC
Chambersburg PA
CBHW030624270326
41927CB00007B/1297